SIGNPOST is a series that aims to reflect the views of the left and help create a common, progressive understanding of issues that matter.

SIGNPOST will address a wide variety of subjects. Each publication in the series shall focus on a single topic that is significant in debates of the day, in a manner that is serious, informative, analytically sound and politically interventionist. The series aims to bring advanced knowledge to the general readers and to activists in movements for social transformation.

SIGNPOST is committed to analyses that are clearly written, attractively produced and moderately priced.

UNCLE SAM'S NUCLEAR CABIN

PRABIR PURKAYASTHA is an engineer and a science activist in the power, telecom and software sectors. He is one of the founding members of the Delhi Science Forum. He is author, along with Vijay Prashad, of *Enron Blowout: Corporate Capitalism and Theft of the Global Commons* (LeftWord 2002).

NINAN KOSHY served on the Commission of the Churches on International Affairs, World Council of Churches (WCC), Geneva, for 17 years. He was Visiting Fellow, Human Rights Programme, Harvard Law School, during 1991–92. He is the author of *Under the Empire: India's New Foreign Policy* (LeftWord 2006) and *The War on Terror: Reordering the World* (LeftWord 2003).

M.K. BHADRAKUMAR served as a career diplomat in the Indian Foreign Service for 3 decades, with postings including India's ambassador to Uzbekistan (1995–98) and to Turkey (1998–2001). He was also posted, in various capacities, at Moscow, Islamabad, Bonn, Colombo, Seoul, Kuwait and Kabul. He is Russian-speaking, and writes regularly on strategic affairs for publications in India and abroad.

SIGNPOST

ISSUES THAT MATTER

PRABIR PURKAYASTHA

NINAN KOSHY

M.K. BHADRAKUMAR

UNCLE SAM'S NUCLEAR CABIN

LeftWord

Other titles in the series

SIGNPOST 1	N. Ram, *Riding the Nuclear Tiger*
SIGNPOST 2	Praveen Swami, *The Kargil War*
SIGNPOST 3	A.G. Noorani, *The RSS and the BJP: A Division of Labour*
SIGNPOST 4	Vijay Prashad, *War Against the Planet: The Fifth Afghan War, Imperialism, and Other Assorted Fundamentalisms*
SIGNPOST 5	A.G. Noorani, *Islam and Jihad*
SIGNPOST 6	Prabir Purkayastha and Vijay Prashad, *Enron Blowout: Corporate Capitalism and Theft of the Global Commons*
SIGNPOST 7	Vijay Prashad, *Namaste Sharon: Hindutva and Sharonism under US Hegemony*
SIGNPOST 8	Archana Prasad, *Environmentalism and the Left: Contemporary Debates and Future Agendas in Tribal Areas*
SIGNPOST 9	Prakash Karat, *Subordinate Ally: The Nuclear Deal and India–US Strategic Relations*

Offset edition first published November 2007.
Reprinted January 2008, April 2009.
Digital print edition, January 2020.

LeftWord Books
2254/2A Shadi Khampur
New Ranjit Nagar
New Delhi 110008
INDIA

leftword.com

LeftWord Books is a division of
Naya Rasta Publishers Pvt. Ltd.

ISBN 978-81-87496-74-8

Contents

PRABIR PURKAYASTHA

COMING OUT OF THE NUCLEAR COLD

The India-US nuclear deal is today the pivot on which the entire range of relations between the two countries turn. While the Indian government is at pains to portray it as a standalone deal limited to cooperation in the area of civilian nuclear energy, the United States has repeatedly emphasized the importance of this deal to the larger India-US strategic relationship. The US needs a reliable strategic ally to help it accomplish its goals in the Asian region, and India, with its large market, is of added commercial interest to the US and its multinational corporations (MNCs).

In order to understand the deal itself, we will have to briefly remind ourselves of India's refusal to be a signatory to the Nuclear Non-Proliferation Treaty (NPT) of 1968, and its subsequent nuclear explosion of 1974. Both these structured a global response of isolating India on nuclear issues and putting it under technology sanctions. The sanctions regime continued to be strengthened by at least three further steps: with the formation of the Nuclear Suppliers Group (NSG) in 1975;[1] the Missile Technology Control Regime (MTCR) in 1987;[2] and the

Wassenaar arrangement in 1996.[3] Each of these was an attempt to create a regime in which sensitive and dual use technologies would be unavailable to some countries. "Sensitive" technologies are those which are directly related to military use, fuel enrichment, reprocessing or heavy water production, while "dual use" technologies are those used in these processes but could have uses outside nuclear applications as well.

India saw the NPT as being discriminatory and refused to sign it. It also went ahead and tested nuclear devices in 1974 and again in 1998. It was obvious that the nuclear powers, led by the US, would seek to isolate India through the nuclear technology control regime. What is not often realised though, is that the regime itself is much broader than the military aspect of it and covers a range of technologies that are termed "dual use."

The NPT divides the world's nations into three groups. The first comprises countries that had developed nuclear weapons by 1968 – the US, USSR (now Russia), China, France, Britain. Though Israel is not a nuclear weapons state by NPT's definition, it occupies the same position in the US's scheme as a formal nuclear weapons state and has never faced sanctions of any kind. The second group comprises those countries which have agreed not to develop nuclear weapons and can be allowed to have different levels of access to nuclear technology for non-military purposes – they include, for instance, Germany and Sri Lanka. The third group comprises countries which are NPT signatories, but the US considers them enemy or rogue states and are therefore not to be allowed access to technology for the nuclear fuel cycle and long and medium range missile systems – Iran is the latest instance.

India is not on the US list of "rouge states," but because of its refusal to sign the NPT, was effectively part of the third group and was denied not only technology for the nuclear fuel cycle and missile development, but also access to all nuclear fuel and reactors. What the Indo-US nuclear deal hopes to do is create a somewhat ambiguous new category, nestled between the first and the second groups – that of a non-rogue, but *de facto* nuclear state, which needs to be brought into the non-proliferation regime with some adjustments to the NPT ground rules.

TECHNOLOGY CONTROL REGIMES

The main thrust of these technology control regimes is that they not only bar specific equipment that could be used in nuclear, missile or military programmes; they are also blanket bans and bar the technology that could produce or help develop equipment that can be used for such purposes. This is what makes the technology sanctions so pernicious. Thus import of all advanced chip manufacturing equipment and supercomputers are deemed dangerous and hence barred to countries such as India.

The current technology control regimes, constructed by the United States and its allies, are as follows:

- Nuclear Materials: Nuclear Suppliers Group (NSG);
- Missiles: Missile Technology Controls Regime (MTCR);
- Chemical and Biological Weapons: Australia Group (AG); and
- Dual Use Technology and Conventional Weapons: The Wassenaar Arrangement (WA).

As the weapons control regimes seek to control the design, development, production and testing of weapon systems, not only are all systems and sub-systems controlled, but all materials, components, design tools such as high speed computers and software, production equipment such as advanced machine tools and various test equipment are also controlled for the target countries. However, all such technologies have very large civilian applications as well. For instance, electronic devices for triggering nuclear devices are also used in oil exploration. Chemicals used to make nerve gas are also used for making plastics. A modern pharmaceutical industry facility could be used to make biological weapons. High-speed computers that are required for climate modelling or designing any modern equipment could also be used to design nuclear bombs. In effect, the above weapons control regimes thus impose a virtual autarchy for the target countries in high technology areas.

Earlier, the NATO countries and their allies controlled flow of advanced technology to the socialist countries under COCOM guidelines, a private arrangement between the NATO countries and Japan. In the post-Cold War period, the COCOM has been broadened in terms of target countries and expanded by inducting countries such as Russia in an agreement known as the Wassenaar Arrangement. By this, a common list of dual use technologies is sought to be banned from export to specific countries and specific entities within certain countries.

SANCTIONS, NON-PROLIFERATION AND DISARMAMENT

The technology sanctions following the 1974 tests had an enormous impact on India's nuclear energy programme. In 1974, India was in the process of building CANDU reactors and heavy water plants with Canadian help but the technology had not been transferred and suddenly all the foreign companies and organizations walked off the project.[4] Those who deride the Department of Atomic Energy (DAE) for its failure to deliver the promised nuclear reactors, have very little idea of how difficult it was for India to continue with its civilian energy programme. Contrary to popular belief, it is much simpler to build a nuclear weapon than it is to build a nuclear reactor. The key issue in building a bomb is getting enough fissile material together. Once that is secured, building the bomb itself is a relatively simple next step.

On the other hand, building the fuel cycle for generating enriched uranium or building nuclear reactors are far more technologically challenging tasks. The problems are compounded if the technology arrangements suddenly cease midway, as they did in 1974. The DAE and its scientists, along with other leading engineering companies in the country – such as Bharat Heavy Electricals Limited (BHEL), Bharat Heavy Plates and Vessels (BHVP) and Larsen and Toubro (L&T) – had to work very hard to enable India's civilian energy programme. They not only had to reinvent the wheel but also had to pioneer new technologies. Most people don't realise that India's quality controls in the engineering industry and the birth of electronics in India came through the aegis of the DAE.

It is precisely this hard work by an entire generation of the nation's scientists and engineers that ensured that the fresh sanctions imposed in the wake of the 1998 nuclear tests did not hurt the country as much. The impact of these sanctions on both the nuclear energy programme as well as the missile programme was much less than the serious dislocation we suffered in 1974. The reason was simple: India had now developed a strong technology base and indigenous manufacturing capability to be able to counter the international isolation. The power plants that had taken 10–15 years to build earlier were now being built in about 5–6 years. The Indian industry had developed capability in a wide range of dual use and advanced technologies and could compete on equal terms with major international companies. The sanctions regime would henceforth cut both ways; while it would certainly inconvenience the Indian industry, it would also create opportunities for Indian organizations in domestic as well as international markets. Conversely, the sanctions also put certain sectors of the Indian market out of bounds for global MNCs.

Within the NPT regime, the compact between the weapons and non-weapons states was two-fold. On the one hand, non-nuclear weapons countries gave up their right to nuclear weapons on the condition that they would have full access to the technology for peaceful uses of nuclear energy. There were not only no further restrictions, but the compact also placed an obligation on nuclear weapons states to transfer such technology to the non-nuclear weapons states. Article IV of NPT states:

> 1. Nothing in this Treaty shall be interpreted as affecting the inalienable right of all the Parties to the Treaty to develop research, production and use of nuclear energy for peaceful

> purposes without discrimination and in conformity with articles I and II of this Treaty.
> 2. All the Parties to the Treaty undertake to facilitate, and have the right to participate in, the fullest possible exchange of equipment, materials and scientific and technological information for the peaceful uses of nuclear energy. Parties to the Treaty in a position to do so shall also cooperate in contributing alone or together with other States or international organizations to the further development of the applications of nuclear energy for peaceful purposes, especially in the territories of non-nuclear-weapon States Party to the Treaty, with due consideration for the needs of the developing areas of the world.[5]

The other part of the compact was that nuclear weapons states would hold good-faith negotiations on nuclear disarmament. However, since they refused to set a timetable for disarmament, it was clear that the nuclear weapons states, led by the US, had no intention of honouring their part of the nuclear bargain. Henceforth, the discourse shifted from disarmament to non-proliferation. The history of the last 40 years bears testimony to the fact that India was absolutely correct in its assessment that the NPT was not an attempt to rid the world of nuclear weapons, but rather an attempt to freeze a regime under which some countries retained the permanent right to carry nuclear weapons.

By the 1990s though, the non-proliferation regime itself was unravelling. The reason for this was not that non-nuclear weapons states suddenly began hankering after nuclear weapons, but that the US, as the world's sole superpower, believed it was time to impose an even more discriminatory world order. The American position developed along two axes. The first concerned its own use of nuclear weapons. In any case, the US is the only country that has always claimed that it has the right to first strike with nuclear weapons – and it remains the only country to have used the weapons in war, in Hiroshima and Nagasaki. Now, with its strategic goal of permanent dominance in every region of the world, it expanded this assertion to include pre-emptive nuclear strikes against any potential challenge to its dominance, irrespective of whether the alleged challenger is a nuclear weapons state or not. The second new element in the American position was to limit nuclear technology to the weapons states and a few of its trusted allies. This took the form of denying some NPT signatories the right to the nuclear fuel cycle, even though it is explicitly sanctioned by the NPT. The current standoff with Iran is part of this thrust.

Even though they have not fulfilled their part of the nuclear bargain, the US and its allies are now asking the non-nuclear weapons countries to give up their right to the nuclear fuel cycle. Only a few countries defined as advanced countries should have this right. To quote George Perkovich, one of the leading American non-proliferation ideologues, "The Nonproliferation Treaty's vague Article IV right 'to develop research, production, and use of nuclear energy for peaceful purposes' should not be interpreted to endorse additional states' acquiring uranium enrichment or plutonium separation facilities."[6]

While the US ratchets up pressure on countries like Iran, denying them what is legitimately their right, it has simultaneously expended billions of dollars in creating a new generation of nuclear weapons, like the so-called "mini-nukes" or the "bunker buster" earth penetrating bombs. Through programmes such as National Missile Defence (NMD) – enthusiastically welcomed by the Indian government – it has sought to militarize, and ultimately nuclearize, outer space. The US currently spends more than $ 6.5 billion on nuclear weapons – about 50 per cent more than it did on average during the Cold War. And while it demands strict adherence to NPT from everyone else, especially those in West Asia, it continues to shield Israel and its estimated arsenal of 200-300 nuclear bombs.

The problem with a preoccupation with the non-proliferation agenda is that it does not address the question of why non-nuclear weapons states are attracted to nuclear weapons in the first place. If in West Asia, Israel has a monopoly of nuclear weapons, and the US goes about threatening countries with "pre-emptive" strikes (nuclear or otherwise) and "regime change," the subjects of these threats feel the need to develop deterrent capabilities. Nuclear weapons are perceived as a viable option. One could argue that nuclear weapons, in fact, do not lead to deterrence but rather escalation of an arms race, but one has to simultaneously address the legitimate concerns that states have about their security. Faced with two aggressors – Israel and the US – both armed with nuclear weapons, both with long histories of mounting pre-emptive attacks, it is not surprising that other states feel threatened.

The Indo-US nuclear deal has to be placed within the context of the ongoing "re-adjustment" of the NPT regime. In the old days, by questioning the logic of non-proliferation and asserting the need for global disarmament, India was looked upon by the US as a troublemaker. If India were to come under the US nuclear umbrella, the troublemaker would then become a willing ally. That this is already coming to pass, even before the nuclear deal is clinched, is clear from India's two votes against Iran at the International Atomic Energy Agency (IAEA) in 2005 and 2006. While explaining its rationale for the votes against Iran, India did not argue in terms of Iran's acts of omission or commission, but argued that India did not want another nuclear weapons state near its border, thereby implicitly accepting the American argument that Iran should not have the right to enrichment of uranium.[7] It is now admitted from the American side that India's votes against Iran were obtained by arm-twisting.[8] It is not unreasonable to speculate, then, that the Iran-Pakistan-India gas pipeline project, which appears to have been given a quiet burial, has also been a victim of this arm-twisting.

While the strategic as well as commercial interests in offering the nuclear deal to India are clear from the American point of view, it is not clear why India should not have waited a little longer for the contradictions within the NPT to mature. In any case, India's emerging economic clout would have ensured that sooner than later, the US and others would have realised that keeping India out through a technology sanctions regime is to miss out on its huge market. Sheer economic interest would have led to the dismantling of the sanctions regime. By negotiating only with the US and making the US its interlocutor with others, India gives up its manoeuvrability internationally for the dubious gain of ending somewhat earlier a failing sanctions regime. Far from being India's last chance of coming out of nuclear isolation imposed by the sanctions, the nuclear deal is in fact proof of the American recognition that things are changing and that India needs to be engaged with on the nuclear issue if the "readjustment" of the NPT regime is to be successfully carried out.

THE AMERICAN PROMISE

What did the US promise India in the July 18, 2005 Joint Statement of George Bush and Manmohan Singh and subsequently, during Bush's India visit in March 2006 – and what has India actually got via the "123" Agreement and the Hyde Act? This is related to another question: what is the Indian perception of what has been promised by the US?

The July 18, 2005 Joint Statement of George Bush and Manmohan Singh indicated that the US would help India come out of its nuclear isolation:

> . . . as a responsible state with advanced nuclear technology, India should acquire the same benefits and advantages as other such states. The President told the Prime Minister that he will work to achieve full civil nuclear energy cooperation with India as it realizes its goals of promoting nuclear power and achieving energy security.[9]

Many Indian commentators have taken the formulation of India being a country "with advanced nuclear technology" to mean that the US recognizes India to be a nuclear weapons state, even if *de facto*. The unstated assumption is that *de facto* recognition is the first step towards legal recognition. In fact, this is not borne out by what the US has done. All that the US has done is to recognize that India possesses nuclear weapons capability, which cannot be rolled back and therefore cannot be kept out of the global nuclear regime permanently. What the US has *not* done is to recognize India as a nuclear weapons state as defined either by the NPT or by its own laws.

The Left parties had cautioned the UPA government regarding the nuclear deal on two inter-related counts.[10] One was to point out that binding India to the US on foreign policy would have serious consequences for India – for instance, in the eventuality of the US attacking Iran, it would be practically impossible for India not to offer its soil for to US forces as a base for staging the attacks. The second point of caution was to point out that the US would shift goalposts in the process of converting the agreement into actual laws. The Left cautioned that any lifting of sanctions would be hedged by many conditions, and in any case the bulk of the sanctions would not be lifted. The price of this limited lifting of sanctions in the nuclear field would be extracted in the realm of foreign policy – apart, of course, from the economic cost of buying nuclear technology, materials, and reactors, to which we will come later.

What India was looking for was three things: a one-time waiver from the US by which all nuclear sanctions against it would be lifted once and for all; help from the US in getting the Nuclear Supply Group (NSG) to make India-specific exceptions, which would pave the way for the NSG lifting its sanctions on India as well; and fuel supply guarantees, particularly keeping in mind the past experience of Tarapur, in which the US reneged on its earlier 123 Agreement.

Much of the current debate hinges on whether the US has delivered on the promises it made in the Joint Statement in 2005, and again in March 2006. The Indian Prime Minister had given assurances in Parliament based on the Indian government's perception of the Bush Administration's promises. Curiously, what was not acceptable to the Prime Minister in his Parliament speeches was hailed by him as an "honourable deal" once the agreement was signed.[11] The only possible explanation of this is that once the legislative process started in the US, the Indian side did not fully comprehend what was happening. Because if this explanation is not accepted, the only other conclusion one can reach is that the Indian government kept the nation in the dark, deliberately.

THE AMERICAN LEGISLATIVE PROCESS

The US has comprehensive laws in its statuette books since 1954 – the Atomic Energy Act (AEA) of 1954 being the main one – regarding collaboration on nuclear energy. The AEA is a document of more than 550 pages and meticulously lays down what the executive can or cannot do in terms of civil nuclear energy cooperation. It is under Section 123 of the AEA that all civilian nuclear energy cooperation agreements are executed. After NPT and India's first nuclear test in 1974, the US also passed the Nuclear Non-Proliferation Act (NNPA) in 1978, which mandated that all previously-existing 123 Agreements be re-negotiated so that any country not designated a non-nuclear weapons state in the NPT would have to accept full-scope International Atomic Energy Agency (IAEA) safeguards before any export of nuclear materials and technology to them could take place. The NNPA was the direct result of Pokhran I and India was its obvious target. It was under NNPA that Tarapur fuel supplies were cut off. NNPA also had specified that any country testing a bomb after 1978 would automatically come under nuclear sanctions.

The Bush Administration initially wanted a simple act passed in Congress, which would lift the embargo on civilian nuclear co-operation with India in spite of India's 1974 and 1998 tests. Had this proposed act been passed in its original form, India would have been treated on par with any other signatory of the NPT which has accepted full-scope safeguards for all its plants, even though India would keep some part of its programme outside safeguards. The Senate and the House of Representatives both rejected this approach arguing that such an authorization would weaken the Congress's oversight of the executive. While the US Congress welcomed the India-US nuclear deal for the strategic (and commercial) benefits it would bring to the US, it reserved the right to oversee the US President's actions, as well as India's future conduct.

The other major provision of the original proposed Act was that for this one-time waiver, only the President would need to verify the conditions required to be fulfilled by India, and the subsequent 123 proposed by the President would have been automatically considered passed after 90 days lie-in period, unless Congress voted against it with a two-thirds majority. Both houses of the US Congress, however, were clear that they wanted the actual consent to the 123 Agreement to be brought before them and they would have the right to reject it with a simple majority.

The US Congress spent considerable time going over the various clauses of the Act. Two bills were independently piloted by the two Houses – the Senate and the House of Representatives – and finally reconciled by a conference of members drawn from both the Houses. What emerged from this conference, and which was finally passed by the US as an act, is the Hyde Act. Many proponents of the deal from the Indian side have argued that the Hyde Act is of no consequence for India, and that surely India cannot be governed by American laws. What is insufficiently appreciated is that the Hyde Act governs what the American executive can and cannot do and also how the US Congress looks at cooperation with India.[12] Since India is seeking supplies from the US (and others) for its nuclear energy programme, it stands to reason that any legislation that governs this supply at the American end is of critical importance to us. Finally, it must be appreciated that the very "123" Agreement which is being projected as a major triumph of Indian foreign policy, is not only enabled by the Hyde Act, but the act also sets the outer limits of what is permissible under the agreement.

At the outset, the Conference document on the Hyde Act makes clear the basis of the Agreement. To quote:

> With the fading of the Cold War's global divisions and the rise of new challenges such as globalization and trans-national terrorism, there is increasing recognition in both the United States and in India that significant benefits may be obtained from closer cooperation across a broad spectrum of activities and policies. These range from shared strategic interests, such as enhanced stability and security in South Asia and the international system as a whole, to more specific priorities, including greater effectiveness in combating the AIDS epidemic, combating terrorism, and preventing the proliferation of weapons of mass destruction, among others.[13]

Thus, quite explicitly, fighting "trans-national terrorism" and "shared strategic interests" are the basis for the agreement. The Conference document also states that India had committed in the Joint Statement of July 18, 2005 that it would support international efforts to limit the spread of enrichment and reprocessing technologies. The Hyde Act reiterates this in its Clause 104 (b) (5) as a prerequisite to the waiver on sanctions. India's stated stand on Iran had been that the country has the right to complete the fuel cycle, including fuel enrichment. However, the US had, from the outset, read into the Joint Statement the commitment that India would work with the US to limit the spread of the fuel cycle to Iran and against its enrichment plans. It is therefore scarcely a surprise that India did in fact abandon its stated position and voted against Iran in the IAEA.

It is now amply clear that the Indian side viewed the deal quite differently from the US Congress. The UPA government is today trying to pretend that the differences do not exist. As we will show below, this is simply not true.

The supporters of the deal have claimed that the nuclear deal will result in India being recognized as a nuclear weapons state and we will henceforth have the same privileges and obligations as any other nuclear weapons state.[14] The Conference document of the Hyde Act read with the Hyde Act makes clear that this was not the way the US Congress viewed India. The Conference document states that Section 128 of the Atomic Energy Act specifies that non-nuclear weapons states in the NPT have to have full scope safeguards as a prerequisite before receiving nuclear material from the US. Further, "Section 129 also requires the termination of nuclear exports if a non-nuclear weapon state has, among other things, tested nuclear weapons after 1978, which India did in 1998." Referring to the proposed act which was not passed, the document says: "The Administration's proposed legislation would have given the President the authority to permanently waive these provisions for India," but this is precisely what was rejected by both the houses of the Congress. The one-time waiver under Section 129, it is now clear, is for activities before July 18, 2005, and India would continue to be looked upon as a non-nuclear weapons state in the future.[15] A violation of any of the clauses in this section will result in the termination of the agreement. Thus, the Hyde Act is clear that it does not look upon India as a *de jure* nuclear weapons power as claimed by Kapil Sibal and Abhishek Manu Singhvi in their articles.[16] It gives India a free pass for its past "violations" of the NPT regime, allows it to have a section of its nuclear programme outside safeguards, but does not relax the bar of a non-nuclear weapon state in any other way.

This would not be important if it did not impinge on a whole range of other issues. The safeguard regime under IAEA, the repercussions of testing, the right to the fuel cycle and accessing technology plays out differently for nuclear weapons states and non-nuclear weapons states as defined under NPT. The US Atomic Energy Act has different provisions for these two categories of states. The bar on testing that the US insists with India directly follows from the section 129 of the Act, and in the words of the Conference document, further "strengthened in the Conference agreement beyond section 129 of the AEA by a provision that the waiver authority in this legislation terminates with any Indian test." Clause 103 (b) (5) of the Hyde Act states that the policies of the United States will be to "Seek to halt the increase of nuclear weapon arsenals in South Asia and to promote their reduction and eventual elimination." US laws, then, are very clear: if India tests again, all nuclear exports are off and the US will ask for all materials to be returned, as it regards India as a non-nuclear weapons state.

The issue here is not that the US should recognize India as a nuclear weapons state. All nuclear weapons states are illegitimate and should implement good faith disarmament measures. India, too, should roll back its weapons programme. The issue here is simply that the protagonists of the deal are claiming that the US has accorded a *de jure* status of the nuclear weapons state to India, whereas, in fact, nothing of the kind has happened.

The second important issue for India is the permanent waiver. The Indian side had sought from the outset a one-time waiver that would not be subject to an annual evaluation or review. It meant that India would not be on permanent notice for its activities, but would have to satisfy the US Congress or President that it had fulfilled all the prerequisites such as separation of civilian and military facilities and IAEA safeguards for the same. Once this waiver was granted, it would be free to participate as an equal in all nuclear matters.

The Congress, however, had quite a different view of India. If we look at the Conference report, a number of provisions of the Hyde Act, particularly the reporting provision of the US President to the Congress, will become clear. The Conference document says:

> As in the Administration's proposed legislation, H.R. 5682 requires the President to determine that India is upholding its July 18, 2005, commitments as a prerequisite for using his waiver authority. The conferees believe that India's *continued implementation* of those commitments is central to the integrity of our bilateral relationship. Therefore, the bill contains *reporting requirements and a provision that calls for termination of exports in the event of violations of certain commitments.* In addition, the bill seeks to uphold existing

> statutory congressional oversight of US nuclear cooperation and exports. At a time when many countries are considering nuclear energy as a viable and desirable alternative to carbon-based energy sources, careful oversight of its expansion is crucial.[17]

Two interrelated points here are to be noted. One is that India is not being given a permanent waiver and would be held to account for the "continued implementation of [its] commitments," as defined in the Hyde Act and interpreted by the Congress. The other point is that the reporting to Congress is directly connected to termination of the agreement – surely then, this is not as innocuous as being made out in some quarters.

THE INDIAN EXPECTATION

In his speech to Parliament in August 2006, Prime Minister Manmohan Singh had said, "if the final product is in its current form, India will have grave difficulties in accepting these Bills."[18] According to the Prime Minister then, what is acceptable to India, and what is not?

The Prime Minister said: "We seek the removal of restrictions on all aspects of cooperation and technology transfers pertaining to civil nuclear energy – ranging from nuclear fuel, nuclear reactors, to re-processing spent fuel, i.e. all aspects of a complete nuclear fuel cycle. . . . We will not agree to any dilution that would prevent us from securing the benefits of full civil nuclear cooperation as amplified above."

The Hyde Act, on the other hand, makes clear that India can receive nuclear fuel or nuclear reactors but cannot expect to import any technology that could be used for its nuclear fuel cycle. This includes fuel enrichment, fuel reprocessing and heavy water production. The only exception would be multi-national or bi-lateral facilities, in which India may be a participant. It should be noted that dual use technology is not limited to technology for enriching and reprocessing of fuel, but covers a whole gamut of other applications, including electronic chip making, advanced materials, precision machining, etc. In other words, India would not have access to the fuel cycle technology and the current restrictions and trade regimes barring access to dual use technology would continue to stay in place.

The second set of issues pertains to "annual good conduct certificate" that the US President has to issue containing minute details of India's activities in a range of areas. The Prime Minister had said: "The draft Senate Bill requires the US President to make an annual report to the Congress that includes certification that India is in full compliance of its non proliferation and other commitments. We have made it [sic] clear to the United States our opposition to these provisions, even if they are projected as non binding on India, as being contrary to the letter and spirit of the July Statement. We have told the US Administration that the effect of such certification will be to diminish a permanent waiver authority into an annual one. We have also indicated that this would introduce an element of uncertainty regarding future cooperation and is, not acceptable to us."

The Hyde Act uses the word "report" in place of "certification," but the substance of the clause remains the same: that the President of the US has to report to the Congress on India's conduct. Further, as the Prime Minister himself said, to project this as being non-binding on India is to forget that a permanent waiver is being diminished into an annual one. The Hyde Act explicitly states that if India is held to be non-compliant then the Administration will also report whether it is in the US security interest to continue with nuclear commerce. India will then be under permanent notice. As the Prime Minister pointed out, this introduces uncertainty in the agreement.

The third important point that the Prime Minister made was that "We cannot accept introduction of extraneous issues on foreign policy. Any prescriptive suggestions in this regard are not acceptable to us." That is precisely what has come to pass. The Hyde Act seeks to "Secure India's full and active participation in United States efforts to dissuade, isolate, and, if necessary, sanction and contain Iran for its efforts to acquire weapons of mass destruction, including a nuclear weapons capability (including the capability to enrich or process nuclear materials), and the means to deliver weapons of mass destruction."[19] Clearly then, the continuation of the nuclear deal is incumbent upon India's foreign policy being tied to the US. Secondly, it calls for a reversal of the long-held Indian position that an NPT signatory has the right to enrich fuel for its civilian programme. This new US interpretation of NPT to mean denial of the fuel cycle is also contained in other sections of the Hyde Act and demands of India a participation in such "non-proliferation" efforts of the US.

The PM had also stated that the IAEA safeguards must be India-specific and India would not accept the Modified Additional Protocols of IAEA with its highly intrusive regime without suitable modifications. The Hyde Act spells out clearly that there will be no India-specific safeguards, that India must adhere to the Modified Additional Protocol as defined by the IAEA for non-nuclear weapon countries for its civilian programme without modifications. It also lays down that US inspectors would check on India's nuclear programme if IAEA could not do so either due to shortage of resources or due to any other reason. This is contrary to the Prime Minister's statement to Parliament: "We will not accept any verification measures regarding our safeguarded nuclear facilities beyond those contained in an India-Specific Safeguards Agreement with the IAEA. Therefore there is no question of allowing American inspectors to roam around our nuclear facilities."[20] However, since the Hyde Act additionally underlines the US need for end-use monitoring as well, it means that US inspectors would eventually end up "roam[ing] around our nuclear facilities."

The US has consistently shifted the goalposts during the negotiations on the nuclear deal. Two new clauses were inserted into the Hyde Act, both of which pertain to the protection that India's civilian energy programme was supposed to have under the July 2005 agreement if the deal is terminated unilaterally by the US – either because of nuclear tests or due to other clauses in the Act. In the July 2005 agreement and the subsequent Separation Plan, it was agreed that in the event of the US cancelling its obligations to supply fuel, it would help in convening a meeting of friendly countries to take over its fuel supply obligations. It was also agreed that the US would help in building a strategic reserve to run our reactors with imported fuel in the event of such a cancellation. The Prime Minister had assured Parliament that "An important assurance is the commitment of support for India's right to build up strategic reserves of nuclear fuel over the lifetime of India's reactors." This is severely curtailed in the Hyde Act. The Conference document made clear that convening of friends to take over US's fuel supply obligations will only cover market failures and will not apply if US decides to terminate the agreement. In such a case, not only will the US not help in convening such a friendly group within the NSG, but will also actively work with other NSG countries to prevent any further supply to India. Further, the reserve that India had proposed to build up for such an eventuality is also denied: the Hyde Act explicitly bars any reserve other than normal operating reserves required to run its reactors.

This is not a minor issue. After the 1974 Pokhran tests, the US withdrew from its commercial obligations to supply fuel for the two Light Water Reactors that it had supplied Tarapur. India had great difficulty in securing fuel for these reactors, finally getting France to supply the required enriched uranium. Even though the US reneged in its commitments to supply fuel to Tarapur, India was forced by its agreement not to reprocess the spent fuel there, but to hold it in perpetuity in costly cooling ponds and other facilities. The NSG did not exist then, and things were a little easier. If the same scenario repeats itself now, India would have to shut off all the imported reactors, as it would have neither fuel nor the right to reprocess the used fuel. It was to prevent a replay of Tarapur that India had introduced the two provisions in the Indo-US nuclear deal. Both have now been affectively subverted.

Once India is locked into these provisions, it will be next to impossible for India to continue running its civilian nuclear energy programme if the US terminates the agreement. The higher its investment in the nuclear energy programme, the more will India be held hostage on extraneous issues such as foreign policy. Already, the mere promise of a deal has made India bend to the US in IAEA on Iran. This is only the tip of the iceberg. Once the US achieves a lock-in on India's nuclear energy programme, India will find itself compromised on energy security and therefore far more vulnerable to American pressure.

It is clear from the provisions identified in the Hyde Act that it does not conform to what the PM had assured Parliament as acceptable to India. India should have discontinued further negotiations on the nuclear deal and pressed for a change in the Hyde Act. If this were not possible, India should then have considered its options and chalked out its policies. Instead, the Indian government decided to ignore the unfavourable provisions in the Hyde Act and went ahead on negotiations for the 123 Agreement, even though it was now clear that any 123 Agreement would have to take place within the parameters set by the Hyde Act.

THE 123 AGREEMENT

It is interesting that the preamble of the 123 Agreement states, amongst other objectives, that the two sides are "desirous of strengthening the strategic partnership between them." In other words, the deepening of the India-US strategic relationship is built into the nuclear deal itself, even though the UPA government pretends otherwise.

After it became clear that the Hyde Act contained provisions that did not meet the Indian Prime Minister's assurances to Parliament, the Indian government took the disingenuous position that the 123 Agreement would address all issue to India's satisfaction. The final text of the 123 Agreement was worked out by end of July, 2007 and made available to the public after the Cabinet had cleared it. After detailed study, the Left parties issued a critique of the 123 Agreement. It was eminently clear that the problems in the Hyde Act remained intact, and had not been addressed in the 123 Agreement.

The 123 Agreement, being a bilateral agreement, addresses only those issues that have a bearing on each other's conduct. From the Indian perspective, the issues were:

- Access to technology and lifting of sanctions.
- Fuel Security, specially after its experience in Tarapur and in light of the Hyde Act provisions.
- The kind of safeguard regime envisaged, specifically if fuel supply assurances are not kept.
- The impact of terminating the agreement on India's continued civilian energy programme and its obligations even after the agreement is terminated.

For the US side, the key issue was its ability to terminate the agreement at will and its residual obligations if the agreement was terminated.

The Indian Prime Minister's understanding was that through this deal, India would secure full cooperation on civilian nuclear technology, including the complete fuel cycle. It has now been conceded by the PM that India has secured only "forward looking language" on this count.[21] The fuel cycle, including dual use technology, will remain under sanctions. Many commentators do not realise the implications of this restriction. Simply put, any technology that can be used for the fuel cycle, even if it has other uses (therefore "dual use") will either remain out of bounds or go through a cumbersome licensing procedure. Thus a major portion of the technology sanctions regime currently in place will remain even after the deal. Critically, Fast Breeder Reactors (FBR) will be regarded as a part of the fuel cycle and technology sanctions on these will continue, even if India puts them under safeguards.

FBR is a key element in India's civilian energy programme. Since India does not have sufficient uranium, we have adopted the FBR route, which allows the uranium fuel to be used much more effectively. Using the FBR route, the same fuel produces 50 times more energy than "burning" it in a Light Water Reactor (LWR) or Pressurised Heavy Water Reactor (PHWR). The three-phase fuel cycle envisages the use of enriched uranium in PHWRs, then using reprocessed plutonium of the PHWRs along with a thorium blanket in FBRs , and finally plutonium and thorium mix in Advanced Heavy Water Reactors (AHWR). This would allow the much more extensive thorium reserves in the country to be used. However, under the current agreement, FBRs are considered fuel enrichment or reprocessing facilities and therefore will be under technology sanctions, even if they are put in the civilian sector and under safeguards. Therefore, the mainstay of our future nuclear energy programme will remain under technology sanctions.

The Indian side has repeatedly said that this is an agreement between equals. Yet, the fact remains that one side is supposed to receive fuel, reactors and other nuclear materials, and the other side is to supply them. The flow of technology and materials is never designed to go the other way. In this situation, the obligations of the supplying side – the US – are critical if the receiving side – India – is not to be held to ransom in future. The fuel supply assurances and the termination clause therefore are of particular importance to India.

The fuel supply assurance is particularly problematic on two major counts. One is that the US is still talking about amending its domestic laws in the 123 Agreement (Clause 5.6):

> As part of its implementation of the July 18, 2005, Joint Statement the United States is committed to seeking *agreement from the US Congress to amend its domestic laws* and to work with friends and allies to adjust the practices of the Nuclear Suppliers Group to create the necessary conditions for India to obtain full access to the international fuel market, including reliable, uninterrupted and continual access to fuel supplies from firms in several nations.[22]

It is entirely unclear what amendments to which domestic laws is the US "committed to seeking," when these amendments will be actually sought, and what would happen if the US Congress rejects the amendments, just as it rejected the Bill that sought a permanent waiver for India. To date, the Indian government has refused to clarify this issue.

On the one hand, then, the fuel supply assurance contained in the 123 Agreement is itself of dubious value. The other aspect of the fuel supply assurance is whether it will hold good if the agreement itself is terminated. It is difficult to imagine that the US would still help India under an agreement clause when the agreement itself has been terminated. The Hyde Act Conference document makes this clear – the alternate fuel supplies refer to a situation of market failure, not where the US has caused the disruption by terminating the agreement. To believe that the US will help in overcoming the problem it has itself created by terminating an agreement is akin to belief in life after death. On the contrary, it is entirely reasonable to assume that the US would invoke the Hyde Act to work with others to deny India fuel.

The Indian government has been curiously silent on the provisions of the termination clause. Instead, it has focussed on the consultations that will precede termination. If we go through the consultations clause, it simply lays down a procedure for consultation which may or may not be followed: the termination clause makes clear that if either party feels consultation will serve no purpose, they can cease further cooperation. The consultations clause is therefore largely cosmetic and will not help if the US decides to terminate the agreement. And as per the Hyde Act, the termination clause can come into effect on a broad range of issues including India's continued links with Iran.

If the agreement is terminated, India will be obliged to return materials and equipment, and be faced with a stoppage of future supplies. The US will be obliged to pay compensation, but India will still be faced with a huge dislocation, as its power programme will suddenly lose some of the installed capacity. As noted earlier, the higher our investment in nuclear energy based on imported fuel and reactors, the bigger the threat. All that the US needs to do to threaten India's nuclear energy programme is to invoke the annual Presidential reporting to the Congress.

The Indian side has made much of securing consent for reprocessing in the 123 Agreement. However, this is a notional right at present, and is subject to conditions that may emerge in the future. It requires a whole series of steps culminating in a separate 131 Agreement with the US. This future agreement will again have to go through the US Congress. In substance, this is not very different from the earlier 123 Agreement, which also granted India the right to reprocess. In practice, however, the right to reprocess was contingent upon "joint determination" by the two sides, and the US consistently stonewalled this. The US reneged on its commitments, but India never received the joint determination it required to reprocess the fuel. The result is that India, to date, is forced to hold the spent fuel in expensive holding ponds. To believe that the future 131 Agreement will be a painless affair – or that even if painful, it will result in India actually acquiring reprocessing rights – is to forget the current 123 experience, and the continuous shifting of goalposts that has occurred during its negotiations.

In contrast to India's 123 Agreement, the 123 Agreements with Japan and Euratom (set up by the European Commission under the Euratom Treaty for supplying nuclear fuel and related activities) have prior consent for reprocessing *along with* pre-approved activities. In India's case it is more a consent to reach an agreement in the future on reprocessing: "Consultations on arrangements and procedures will begin within six months of a request by either Party and will be concluded within one year."[23] Though the UPA government has projected that it has already secured reprocessing rights, the clause here makes clear that unless the arrangements and procedures are finalized, the right to reprocess remains a notional one.

The Indian side believes that the NSG will give India better terms and unrestricted right to nuclear fuel and technology. However, were this to happen, the American suppliers of reactors and equipment would be at a serious disadvantage in the Indian market. The Conference document in fact voices precisely this concern – that others may give India better terms than the US and this would hurt American commercial interests – and asks the US Administration to make sure this does not happen. Since the NSG works by consensus and the US is supposed to steer India's case there, to imagine that the NSG guidelines will work to the detriment of American commercial interests defies belief.

THE ENERGY ISSUE

The Indian government has argued that there is a serious shortage of electricity in the country and therefore all sources of power need to be exploited. This is doubtless true. However, after the Enron fiasco, surely we must ask: is electricity at any cost to be preferred over shortage? Would it help our agriculture and industry, facing increasing global competition, to be saddled with exorbitantly priced electricity? How are they expected to compete with China or the US when their costs are significantly higher?

Then there is the question of shortage of capital to invest in infrastructure. The Government of India for the last 15 years has not been able to find money to invest in the power sector. In the Seventh Five Year Plan, we had added about 21,000 MW. In the Eighth and Ninth Plans we added 16,422MW and 19,095 MW respectively. In the Tenth Plan, we have added a little more than 20,000 MW. This slowing down of adding to the installed capacity is based on the plea that the government has no money. Therefore, capital crunch has to be factored into any energy policy for the country.

It goes without saying that electricity is only one part – albeit a very important part – of India's infrastructure expansion needs. Just as we need to expand energy supply, we need to build roads, railways, ports, etc. It is in this context that a rigorous evaluation of alternatives becomes important. It is curious that the importance of nuclear energy has suddenly become an issue before the nation in the context of the India-US nuclear deal. If the government sincerely believes nuclear energy to be so critical to India's energy security, why has it not presented a detailed techno-economic study evaluating the costs and benefits of nuclear energy?

At present, we have an installed capacity of about 143,000 MW, with a mixture of coal, hydro, gas and nuclear power. One MW of power can supply electricity equal to the needs of about 8,000–10,000 households. Out of the 143,000 MW that we have installed, electricity based on nuclear power plants is only 4,120 MW, which is less than 3 per cent of our total installed capacity. The major share is coal, which has about 55 per cent of installed capacity followed by Hydro, which is about 25 per cent.

A part of the reason for the low share of nuclear energy has been the nuclear isolation we have faced and therefore the much slower development of our programme. However, this is only a part of the reason. The other part is the techno-economics of nuclear power and its relatively high cost.

Here, it is important to understand the difference between power and energy. Energy is what we use, whether in our electric lights, heaters or air conditioners. Power is the amount of energy produced in one second. Power is measured in KW (Kilo Watts) or MW (Mega Watts). If a pump of 1 KW runs for 1 hour, it then consumes 1 unit of electricity – the units are what you pay for in your electricity bill. The installed capacity of plants is measured in MWs and measures the capability of these plants to produce energy. How much it produces compared to how much it can produce gives us the Plant Load Factor or PLF.

For the foreseeable future, renewable energy sources – wind and solar – are not going to meet our energy needs. Currently, though we have installed about 6,000 MW of wind energy, it must be noted that wind speeds in India are not high and we can at best secure 20 per cent energy from this if we had installed thermal plants (thermal plants burn coal, gas or oil to produce electricity) of the same capacity. That is, if a plant say of 1 MW runs on wind power, in periods that wind speeds are low, it hardly produces any energy. The PLF of wind plants is therefore

TABLE 1 *Planning Commission's Optimistic Nuclear Power Scenario*

	2006	2016	2021
Total Installed Capacity in GW	134.7	303	445
Nuclear Capacity	4.12	15	30
Nuclear as a % of total	3.06	4.95	6.74

Note Figures for 2016 and 2021 are from *Integrated Energy Policy*, Planning Commission, August 2006.

TABLE 2 *Govt's Current Optimistic Nuclear Power Scenario*

	2006	2016	2021
Total Installed Capacity in GW	134.7	303	445
Nuclear Capacity	4.12	20	40
Nuclear as a % of total	3.06	6.60	8.99

Note This table uses the demand figures as in Table 1 and the nuclear energy figures based on claims that the Government is now making of 40,000 MW by 2020.

about 20 per cent, while that of thermal plants is about 70–80 per cent. Thus the 6,000 MW of wind power converted to electrical energy is equivalent to the output from 1,500 MW of thermal power. Therefore, our energy requirements in the short and even medium term have to be largely met from coal, gas, hydro and nuclear sources.

If we assume that we need to add about 100,000 MW in the next 10 years, as the Ministry of Power says, what is the best-case scenario for nuclear power? According to the Planning Commission's study,[24] taking the most optimistic scenario, nuclear energy will contribute 15,000 MW by 2015 and 29,000 MW by 2021 (Table 1). These targets include 8,000 MW of imported reactors. Even though the Planning Commission admits that these targets are quite ambitious (it calls it the "Optimistic Scenario"), let us assume for the sake of argument that they are met. Even then, nuclear energy will only add up to about 7 per cent of our total installed capacity.

With the nuclear deal under intense scrutiny, the Government is going into overdrive now, claiming to be capable of adding 40,000 MW by 2020. This figure has no relation to actual capabilities on the ground, or to the huge capital required to install fresh capabilities, or indeed to the cost of power if plants actually do come up. However, even if one disregards these issues, going by these more than optimistic scenarios, nuclear power would still account for less than 9 per cent of our total installed capacity. In addition, as we will show below, such an ambitious nuclear electricity programme will come at a high cost and will dry up investments in other sectors.

In the 1960s and 1970s, there was a lot of euphoria about nuclear power. By the 80s, it became clear that nuclear power was expensive. In the West, nuclear plants routinely overshot their budgets and the time required to erect them. With discovery of gas in large quantities and increased efficiency of thermal power plants, nuclear plants were perceived to be too expensive. This was quite independent of the debate regarding the potential hazards, de-commissioning costs, and the problem of storing nuclear wastes.

The Indian experience has been no different. Nuclear power plants are about 50 per cent more expensive, even when using domestic technology and equipment. Further, since they take a long time to build, a large amount of capital is locked up during construction. If the plant is built using a mix of equity and debt, this cost of locking up money is known as Interest During Construction (IDC). The capital cost of building a plant, without taking its IDC into account, is called "overnight" cost. All conventional power plants are built with a mixture of debt and equity and this is also the way Nuclear Power Corporation (NPC) proposes to build plants in the future. Taking the debt-equity ratio 70:30 and IDC for both thermal and nuclear plants, the capital cost of nuclear power plants would be twice that of coal-based thermal power plants – about Rs 7.4 crore per MW (about Rs 6.2 crore as overnight costs and 6 years to construct the plants) for nuclear plants, as against Rs 3.73 crore per MW for coal fired plans (Rs 3.3 crore as overnight costs and 4 years' time for construction). Simply put, this means that for the cost incurred in putting up nuclear plants that will generate 10,000 MW of nuclear power we can put up coal-fired plants to generate 20,000 MW.

If imported reactors for nuclear power are considered, the figures become even more unfavourable. The overnight cost of nuclear plants is Rs 9 crore per MW. A number of studies have taken this as the base cost of nuclear power plants. Though the nuclear plant suppliers have claimed a lower figure, all existing plants have cost more than $ 2,000 per KW and therefore this is a reasonable base for our calculations. As the *Business Week* pointed out, "the cheapest plants built recently, all outside the US, have cost more than $ 2,000 per kilowatt."[25] Taking into account the IDC component, this translates to Rs 11.2 crore per MW or *three times the cost of coal-fired power plants*. In other words, with the same amount of money, we could put up 30,000 MW of coal-fired power plants instead of 10,000 MW of imported nuclear plants. For a 40,000 MW nuclear power programme, if we import 30,000 MW of imported reactors with 10,000 MW of indigenous reactors, it means an investment of Rs

TABLE 3 *Comparison of Capital Costs and Tariffs, Coal vs. Nuclear*

	Coal 2 units of 500 MW	*Gas 1000 MW*	*Hydro 1000 MW*	*Nuclear 2 units of 500 MW (domestic)*	*Nuclear 1,000 MW (imported)*
Capital cost/MW without IDC (Rs crore)	3.3	2.635	4.5	6.2	9.0
Construction period (months)	48	36	96	72	72
Capital cost/MW with IDC (Rs crore)	3.73	3.0	7.1	7.4	11.2
Capital cost without IDC (Rs crore)	3,300	2,635	4,500	6,000	9,000
Capital cost with IDC (Rs crore)	3,757	3,000	7,100	7,736	11,229
Tariff per unit (Rs)	2.37	2.44	2.5	3.6	4.6

Note 1 See http://www.uic.com.au/nip08.htm for nuclear fuel costs.

Note 2 An earlier version of the calculations[26] above had used figures, which were based on slightly different capital costs and a 10-year loan repayment period. The modified calculations uses 14 year loan repayment period with interest charges of 11.5 per cent and a discounting rate of 11.1 per cent.

TABLE 4 *Cost of Nuclear and Coal Based Power Stations*

	Capital cost of coal fired plant (Rs crore)	*Capital cost of nuclear plant with domestic PWR reactors (Rs crore)*	*Capital cost of nuclear plant with imported LWR reactors (Rs crore)*
1 MW	3.73	7.4	11.1
10,000 MW	37,300	74,250	11,1380
40,000 MW	149,200	297,000	445,500

410,000 crore, which is more than the total amount of investment we have currently planned for the entire 100,000 MW of the next 10 years. Incidentally, India's total capacity addition in the last 10 years has been less than 40,000 MW, the figure that is now being proposed for nuclear power alone.

The cost of power from nuclear plants, as compared to that from coal-fired plants, is also substantially higher. Coal-fired plants today produce electricity at the plant end (not as delivered to the consumer) at about Rs 2.20–Rs 2.50 per unit depending on the coal cost at the location. For nuclear plants with domestic reactors, the cost is about Rs 3.60 per unit. For imported reactors, it is about Rs 4.60 per unit. If we assume time for construction to be 8 years instead of 6, as is quite likely for imported reactors, then the corresponding cost figures would be more than Rs 5.00 for imported units.

A Congress party spokesperson has claimed that domestic nuclear reactors with a capital cost of Rs 6.5 crore, will produce power at the cost of only Rs 2.50 per unit in five to six years.[27] This, it is claimed, is lower than that of a coal-fired plant at a load centre. If this were indeed the case, then how do we explain that power from Kaiga Atomic Power Station costs around Rs 3.50 based on the same value of capital costs that Singhvi has assumed? In fact, the NPC's figures show the cost to be Rs 3.83 per unit; the NPC claims that it is subsidising Kaiga power by charging only Rs 3.50. Plants write-off their capital costs with time and therefore if we want to compare cost of electricity from different type of plants, we must take plants of the same vintage. An older thermal plant such as Singrauli or older nuclear plants such as Tarapur 1&2 produce electricity at 78 paise and 95 paise respectively, as they have written off their capital costs. However, if we compare the cost of supply from nuclear stations to that of coal-fired plants of the same vintage, the nuclear costs are always higher than that from any coal-fired plant anywhere in the country, irrespective of its location.

As the cost of nuclear energy is largely from its capital cost, the cost of electricity from imported reactors at Rs 9 crore per MW will be at least twice that from equivalent-sized thermal plants. The cost of electricity using imported coal in Mundra project is Rs 2.26 per unit. The Sasan project, which is at pithead and therefore has a lower cost of fuel, is around Rs 1.19 per unit. Even gas-based units at much higher gas costs of $ 4–5 per million BTU, would produce power at Rs 2.50–Rs 3.00 per unit. These are half the cost of electricity from imported reactors. How, then, do we justify importing such costly reactors?

Then there are other questions, related to the growth and development of our own nuclear energy establishment. We have built an indigenous nuclear industry, which can today meet the demands of manufacturing and installing nuclear plants in the country. Importing reactors means starving our domestic industry of orders and placing these orders on foreign suppliers. Therefore, the multiplier effect in the domestic economy for supplying equipment in terms of orders and jobs would not take place. Instead, such orders would flow to countries abroad. For the nuclear industry in the US, which has not received a new domestic order for the last nearly 30 years, a booming Indian market may act to revive it.[28] Should this be our objective or should we use our investments in the energy sector to increase our own manufacturing base?

The Planning Commission documents, as well as a host of independent studies, accept that comparative costs favour coal and domestic gas over nuclear power. This is not to argue that nuclear energy, as an option, should not be pursued. On the contrary, given the long-term scenario, nuclear energy, particularly our indigenous fast breeder and thorium programme, remains the only realistic source for the *future*, if solar energy does not pan out. But how much nuclear energy to use *today* has to be based primarily on the techno-economics of different sources of energy.

Singhvi and others have warned us of impending huge shortages by 2032, because "even an 8 per cent average annual GDP [growth] requires 1 million MW," and that using all other sources of energy, "we cannot cross a maximum of 4 lakh MW." This, Singhvi says, would leave an uncovered deficit of at least half of our needs. However, the *Integrated Energy Policy* document of the Planning Commission has worked out *11 different scenarios* for meeting the total requirements of installed capacity by 2031–32. *Not one* of these scenarios has an uncovered deficit of *any* amount. And the highest amount of nuclear energy the Commission has included in these scenarios is achieved by adding only 63,000 MW of nuclear plants – or less than 8 per cent of the total installed capacity. How then do we understand Singhvi's figures?

To justify the nuclear deal, Singhvi and others have constructed a huge but imaginary shortfall in the year 2031–32, then zeroed in on nuclear energy – that too with imported reactors – as the only path to salvation. Once this calamitous future of enormous shortages is created, it's that much easier to rush the country into hasty decisions. This method is not new; the Congress and the Bharatiya Janata Party spokespersons had used the same method to justify the Enron deal. And everyone knows what we got out of *that* deal.[29]

Let us look at alternative energy sources. Coal can definitely sustain an energy programme of many times its current size for the next 50–100 years. Hydro potential is estimates to be 150,000 MW, out of which we have used only about 18 per cent. Further hydro potential can be tapped if we are able to work jointly with other Himalayan countries. Though hydro has serious problems of dislocation and rehabilitation of those displaced, nevertheless it is a source that cannot be eschewed given our future needs. Gas has now been discovered in the Kaveri-

Godavari Basin in large quantities and also in other places. A gas-based programme can support 50,000 to 75,000 MW. So the nuclear option is not the only option for the country, as the Government has suddenly started to claim.

Not only is nuclear power more expensive, particularly with imported reactors, investing in nuclear power in a big way without addressing its techno-economics will also have adverse effects on the entire electricity sector. Going in for huge investments for imported nuclear power plants – three times the cost of similar coal-fired units – would mean starving the Indian economy of other investments. It would mean either giving up much larger investments in the power sector or starving other infrastructure sectors.

THE NUCLEAR INDUSTRY

The Left opposition to the nuclear deal, or its critique of the techno-economics of nuclear power, should not be construed to mean that the Left is unequivocally opposed to nuclear power *per se*. On the contrary, the Left has argued that India must invest in nuclear technology. Because of the severe sanctions they faced, India's nuclear scientists and technologists struggled very hard to develop every bit of our nuclear technology indigenously. This technology has been hard-earned, and needs now to be nurtured and developed further.[30] In the long run, as coal and oil reserves become scarcer, nuclear technology is likely to become more and more important. However, to argue that we should put a major part of our available resources into nuclear energy today – to the benefit of American suppliers, not our own indigenous industry – seems very short sighted indeed.

The last nuclear reactor commissioned in the US was in 1996, and it had taken 23 years to build. What had killed the nuclear power industry in the US is neither the hazards of nuclear power nor the question of disposing nuclear wastes, but quite simply its cost. It was way too expensive to put up nuclear power plants and the electricity out of it cost much more than from other sources. The US nuclear industry today survives almost entirely on foreign orders. And that is why they are looking to India for orders worth billions to revive their moribund industry.

For those who recall the Enron fiasco, there is a definite sense of *déjà vu*. The decision to award Enron a 2,000 MW project was a political decision. Then, we found our fuel and power policies being changed to suit Enron. The liquid fuel policy of using naphtha fuel for power plants came out of the need to accommodate Enron. Today, it is clear that such a policy, implemented without application of mind and the techno-economics of the sector, has resulted in a major crisis for the Maharashtra State Electricity Board (MSEB) and idling of plants using naphtha. Unfortunately, a similar exercise is underway with respect to nuclear energy. If the MSEB crisis was the result of adding a 2,000 MW Enron plant, we can only imagine what would be the impact of introducing 40,000 MW and its high cost power.

The talk of using imported nuclear reactors for providing energy security is also misleading. Unlike the three-phase nuclear cycle, which envisages the use of enriched uranium in Pressurised Water Reactors (PWR), then using reprocessed plutonium of the PWRs in Fast Breeder Reactors (FBR), and finally plutonium and thorium mix in Advanced Heavy Water Reactors (AHWR), the imported Light Water Reactors (LWR) plants use only enriched uranium. In such a cycle, the requirements of uranium are much higher, and we would need continuous imports of large amounts of uranium. If we concentrated, instead, on the FBR and AWHR route, this would require much smaller amounts of uranium and would provide much greater fuel security than the imported reactor route that the Government is currently pushing.

One of the objectives of the US through this deal is also provide an immediate "easy" LWR route to India for nuclear energy instead of developing FBR technology. It is interesting that it is only when the Department of Atomic Energy has been able to commercialize its PWR technology and scale it up to 540 MW that the US is now offering to lift technology sanctions on

TABLE 5 *Approximate Potential Available From Domestic Sources for Nuclear Energy*

	Amount (Tonnes)	*Electricity*	
		Electrical Energy (GWYr)	*Power (MW)*
Uranium-metal	61,000		
In PWR		330	10,000
In FBR		42,200	500,000
Thorium-metal (in breeders)	2,25,000	1,50,000	very large

Source Department of Atomic Energy, quoted in *Integrated Energy Policy, 2006*, Planning Commission, p. 36.

reactors and fuel. Once we take this easy route, they will then be able to control us through their control over fuel as well as control over technology (spare parts, etc.). Therefore, developing the FBR route and indigenous reactor technology would provide a much surer route to energy security than taking the dependent route of imported reactors.

Electricity is only a part of our total energy needs. We need fuel for transport and also for manufacturing fertilisers and petrochemicals. The requirements of primary fuels would of course also depend partially on what kind of fuel we use for electricity generation. However, it is clear that in any scenario, the bulk of India's electricity needs – from 91 per cent as the best-case scenario to 95 per cent as per current plans – would have to come from non-nuclear sources. For the foreseeable future, the nuclear option is going to have little impact on our need for other sources of energy.

Oil has been used in India primarily for transport and industry. The Tenth Plan has this to say about the growth of hydrocarbon demand:

> The share of hydrocarbons in the primary commercial energy consumption of the country has been increasing over the years and is presently estimated at 44.9 per cent (36.0 per cent for oil and 8.9 per cent for natural gas). The demand for oil is likely to increase further during the next two decades. The transportation sector will be the main driver for the

> projected increase in oil demand. Consequently import dependence for oil, which is presently about 70 per cent, is likely to increase further during the Tenth and Eleventh Plans.[31]

It has been estimated that by 2015, Indian demand for crude oil would be around 4.25–4.5 million barrels/day (mb/d) and it would be importing about 80 per cent of this, almost entirely from the West Asian region. The important issue here is that if we look at the power sector demand, oil does not figure in this. So nuclear energy, which can be used to produce electricity, is not a substitute for oil under any circumstances. While India accounts for only about 2 per cent of world's oil consumption, it is already amongst the 10 largest importers of oil in the world. With increasing oil consumption, this trend is likely to continue with India and China emerging as major importers of oil, accounting for at least 15 per cent of world's oil demand. As there is no way nuclear energy can go into trucks, buses and cars, the transport sector will continue to be heavily dependent on imported hydrocarbons.

If we take nuclear energy as a fraction of the total primary energy needs of the country, we find that this is not more than 3–5 per cent of our total primary energy basket (the 5–9 per cent of the electrical energy translates to 3–5 per cent in primary energy terms). If we look at oil and gas, even with an ambitious nuclear energy programme, they will constitute more than 30 per cent and 10 per cent respectively, and together more than 40 per cent of our future energy needs.

Therefore, the India-US nuclear deal will help us address our primary energy needs only marginally. The argument that nuclear energy is the energy for the future is not backed up by either an analysis of India's energy needs nor does it take into account that nuclear energy is an option very few countries are exercising today. We definitely need to keep the nuclear option open, looking at possible long-term needs; but to present this as a panacea for our current energy requirements flies in the face of reality. If India has to take measures for its energy security, its primary concern must be to secure oil and gas supplies.[32] It is in this context that peace and stability in West Asia are of such vital concern for India. Its delight in being seated at the international high table, courtesy the US, is a harmful diversion that is against our national interests.

DISARMAMENT AND NPT

From the Nehru period down to Rajiv Gandhi, India stood for nuclear disarmament. It opposed the NPT regime as a discriminatory one that allowed the nuclear weapons states to maintain and even augment their nuclear arsenals while preaching the virtues of abstinence to others. The phrase "nuclear apartheid" originates from India's view of the NPT regime. It was in June 1988 that Rajiv Gandhi, addressing the UN General Assembly, had proposed a bold plan for nuclear disarmament:

> Nuclear war will not mean the death of a hundred million people. Or even a thousand million. It will mean the extinction of four thousand million: the end of life as we know it on our planet earth. We come to the United Nations to seek your support. We seek your support to put a stop to this madness.[33]

Even during the Comprehensive Test Ban Treaty (CTBT) discussions, India had indicated a willingness to sign the treaty if the nuclear weapons states were willing to give a definite timetable for disarmament.

It was under the BJP-led government that the first shift in position on NPT and disarmament took place. Post 1998, the argument was advanced that India's opposition to NPT was merely because it was not accepted as a nuclear weapons state. This is exactly what India's critics had earlier argued: that India was essentially hypocritical in its opposition to NPT. The infamous train compartment argument, that those inside do not want anyone from outside to get in, was advanced on why India was now agreeing to sign on to the NPT regime as a nuclear weapons state. The UPA government under Manmohan Singh has continued this line, with only lip service to disarmament.[34] India is now in the same company as the nuclear weapon states, proclaiming disarmament but practicing non-proliferation.

The 123 Agreement is the first international agreement in which India is formally accepting the goal of non-proliferation. The Preamble to the 123 Agreement states, amongst other things, that the two signatories are "mindful of their shared commitment to preventing the proliferation of weapons of mass destruction."

Non-proliferation is no longer taboo or an expression of nuclear apartheid. India is willing to join the American bandwagon to promote non-proliferation. From an opponent of non-proliferation, India has now become its latest champion. It has abandoned the non-aligned world, which has always argued that nuclear weapons states should pursue good faith negotiations for disarmament.

India now believes, along with a handful of nuclear weapon states, that the goal of nuclear disarmament is a distant one. However, the reality is that this goal cannot be put on the back burner anymore. Nuclear weapons are a dangerous and a persistent threat to the existence of all life on the planet. The argument that the proliferation firewall can be held indefinitely is a dangerous illusion. As the technology of the fuel cycle becomes easier to acquire, it is impossible that the regime of technology controls that the US is proposing and India has now joined, will continue to hold. It is only the very short-sighted who believe that a complex system of sanctions and restrictions will allow the continuation of nuclear weapons in the hands of only a few countries. By this, they are courting global disaster as it is only driving other countries down the path of acquiring nuclear weapons. Even a completely amoral proponent of the realist school of national interest such as Henry Kissinger, is now arguing for immediate measures for nuclear disarmament.[35] The realisation is slowly sinking in that the regime christened as "nuclear apartheid" by India cannot be maintained indefinitely.

Either the US and other nuclear weapons states take steps to disarm, or there will be many more declared and undeclared nuclear weapon states. If this eventuality comes to pass, the world will become an infinitely more dangerous place.

It is at this time that India needs to show imagination and its commitment to peace. This is the time for showing global leadership. India has an honourable record and a nuclear capability that had weathered isolation. Its call for disarmament would have been heard. This is how countries become great, by understanding the moment and seizing it.

Instead, the current Indian leadership has seized of the US coattails hoping that will make them global leaders. It is the ultimate irony that the current Congress leadership is thinking of aligning with the US to become a global power, when admittedly it is already an economic power. They forget that India became a leader in the international community by virtue of championing nuclear disarmament, de-colonization, opposition to apartheid, and support for national liberation causes. All this, at a time that it was economically far weaker.

If India wanted to break out of its nuclear isolation, was this the only way? India basically needed nuclear fuel. The technology sanctions regime cannot be continued forever and it is not unreasonable to argue that it would have broken in a few years in any case, if India had been patient. For securing nuclear fuel, a much better strategy would have been to engage with the other countries that are also members of the NSG and not just restrict this engagement to the US. This would have preserved our policy of non-alignment, while not compromising on disarmament.

If we take stock of what is happening, it is clear that India stands to lose more than it will gain from the deal. India becomes a junior partner in the US strategic scheme, the technology embargoes stay, it becomes a party to the even more discriminatory fuel cycle programme of the US, renounces cheap gas from Iran, all for the sake of choosing an expensive and dependent route for development of nuclear energy. Which, in any case, is of marginal importance in the energy scenario. Self respect demands that India renounces this subservient path of "strategic partnership" with the US and reasserts its independent foreign policy. The people cannot let a minority government abandon the nation's long-held positions of an independent foreign policy for the dubious benefit of a seat at the high table, courtesy the US.

NINAN KOSHY

INDIA-US NUCLEAR DEAL: THE BROADER PICTURE AND WIDER IMPLICATIONS

The US-India civilian nuclear deal has emerged as the most important political issue of our times, polarizing the country in an unprecedented manner. Hailed by the Congress Party as "the greatest national event in keeping with the highest legacy of diplomacy,"[1] the nuclear deal is billed as the outstanding achievement of the UPA government. However, a careful analysis of the background and context of the deal will clearly show that if operationalized, it will severely undermine India's independence in foreign policy and defence.

The text of the "Agreement for Cooperation between the Government of India and the Government of the United States of America Concerning Peaceful Uses of Nuclear Energy" was released simultaneously in Washington and New Delhi on August 3, 2007. To understand the broader picture and wider implications of the deal, one has to go back to the significant developments in the first half of 2006 leading to the July 18 Joint Statement of President George W. Bush and Prime Minister Manmohan Singh.

PARTNERSHIP IN THE IMPERIAL COALITION

"It is official. It is the policy of the United States to help India to become a major world power in the 21st century. This is what Secretary of State Condoleezza Rice conveyed to Prime Minister Singh during her visit to India," announced the American Ambassador to India, David C. Mulford.[2] However, Rice stated in New Delhi in March 2005 and later in Washington as well, that this "major world power" groomed by the United States would not have Washington's support for a permanent seat in the UN Security Council. In other words, what was being offered was a permanent place in the grand imperial coalition.

During her New Delhi visit Rice clarified a few other matters as well. Washington's preference was to its own initiatives on global security to that of the UN, and it wanted India to align more closely with the US rather than the UN. It was made clear that India's relations with countries which were "against the USA" were subject to the approval by Washington. India's role in the world was to be defined in the framework of the American imperium – not by India and not in the framework of the UN. While making noises about independence in foreign policy for domestic consumption, there is every reason to believe that the Indian leadership accepted the US conditions to help India to become a major world power. A US State Department briefing elaborated the announcement on helping India by saying that Washington understood "fully the implications including the military implications of that statement."

Leaders and senior officials of the USA have repeatedly stated from September 2001, when India declared whole-hearted supported to its War on Terror, that the India-US relationship is essentially a military relationship on American terms and primarily in American interests. The Framework Agreement on Defence Cooperation signed on June 28, 2005, in Washington by Defence Secretary Donald Rumsfeld and Defence Minister Pranab Mukherji was clear evidence of this. Moreover this Agreement confirmed that India accepted fully the conditions laid down by the US to help India become a major world power.

Subsequent developments have shown that this Agreement was crucial in shaping the India-US nuclear deal.

The Agreement said that the two countries were entering a new era and transforming the relationship "to reflect on common principles and shared national interests." It stated that "defence relationship would support and be part of the larger bilateral strategic partnership . . . conducting joint exercises and exchanges and collaborating in multinational operations." Strengthening the militaries' capabilities to combat proliferation of weapons of mass destruction and expanding collaboration in missile defence are important parts of the Agreement. Expansion of defence trade finds a prominent place in the Framework.

The Agreement goes far beyond defence matters. Several of the provisions go against the tenets of India's foreign policy. These clauses include "collaboration in multinational operations," "expanding collaboration in missile defence" and assisting in "building world wide capacity to conduct successful peacekeeping operations." "Collaboration in multi-national operations" deserves a special note. US officials have repeatedly mentioned the objective of Indian and American military joining in ope-rations in third countries. In US strategic parlance "multinational operation" means US-led military operation outside the purview of the authorization or permission of the United Nations. Simply put, this means imperial wars. Participation in such wars is what India has agreed to.

The Agreement, with its far-reaching consequences, is by far the most important pact made with the US by India. The Indian public was kept in the dark about such a major agreement and there was no hint that such a momentous compact would be made during the visit of the Indian Defence Minister to Washington in June 2005. In fact on the eve of his visit he downplayed its significance, saying that the trip was "exploratory in nature." Considering the significant role the Agreement had in the making of the nuclear deal, it is evident that there was a deliberate move on the part of New Delhi to keep away from public scrutiny the links between different parts of the strategic alliance.

It is important to note that the Defence Agreement was made just twenty days before the much-heralded Joint Statement of July 18, and in fact provided its basis. It was the condition precedent for the nuclear deal. The Joint Statement stated, "India would be ready to assume the same responsibilities and practices and acquire the same benefits and advantages as other leading countries with advanced nuclear technologies such as the United States." These responsibilities and practices consist of "identifying and separating civilian and nuclear facilities and programmes in a phased manner"; "filing a declaration on its civilian facilities with the International Atomic Energy Agency"; taking a decision "to place voluntarily its civilian nuclear facilities under IAEA safeguards"; continuing India's unilateral moratorium on nuclear testing; supporting international non-proliferation efforts through a comprehensive export control legislation; adhering to the guidelines of the Missile Technology Control Regime and the Nuclear Suppliers' Group; and "refraining from transfer of enrichment and reprocessing technologies to states that do not have them."

The Joint Statement, which is often presented as dealing only with the civilian nuclear deal, begins by declaring the American President's and the Indian Prime Minister's interest "to transform the relationship between their two countries and establish a global partnership." It specifically "expressed satisfaction at the New Framework for the US-India Relationship as a basis for future cooperation."[3]

The Joint Statement showed that India gave undertakings which were against its long-standing policies on nuclear issues. The conditions that India accepted were essentially those of international treaties, especially the Comprehensive Test Ban Treaty and the Non-Proliferation Treaty, which India had hitherto refused to sign or adhere to. The commitment to identify and separate civilian and military facilities and programmes and allow international inspection of civilian facilities was a major change from the policy followed for more than forty years.

It appeared that the Indian Prime Minister agreed to another condition as well – to ditch the pipeline deal with Iran. In proposing an "energy dialogue" with India when she was in New Delhi in March 2005, Secretary of State Rice was the first explicitly to link US flexibility on the nuclear question to the Iran pipeline. Siddharth Varadarajan wrote, "Washington delivered on its promise on the nuclear front. If the new US-India defence framework took New Delhi upto the door, the key to unlocking lay in the safeguards and test ban concessions India made. What is left now is the implementation. And India has been told in no uncertain terms that if Congress is to legislate the changes President Bush has committed – he could have used a Presidential waiver but chose not to – the pipeline deal with Iran must not go through."[4]

Dr A.N. Prasad, former Director of the Bhaba Atomic Energy Research Centre (BARC), said that segregation of civilian and military facilities in India is "impossible." For India, he said, going down the road of stockpiling – which is what the logic of the India-US Joint Statement implies – would be "highly counterproductive."

The Joint Statement was a virtual abdication of India's principled nuclear disarmament policy. As the Polit Bureau of the CPI (M) pointed out , for decades India "was committed to nuclear disarmament. The Rajiv Gandhi plan for disarmament was the last major initiative taken in this regard. The BJP-led government had begun the journey of accepting junior partnership of the US in return for a *de facto* recognition as nuclear weapon state. . . . The current agreement marks an end to India's nuclear disarmament policy."

A series of developments followed in fairly quick succession after the Joint Statement of July 18, 2005: the visit of President Bush at the beginning of March 2006; the acceptance of the separation plan; legislative actions in the US Congress and Senate culminating in the Hyde Act; and negotiations in New Delhi and Washington.

During the last two years the attention of the Prime Minister and the foreign policy establishment seems to have been entirely focused on Washington and fully preoccupied by the great joint enterprise with President Bush. In doing so, they were occasionally sidelining, if not ignoring, other opportunities and risks in foreign affairs. Even when dealing with other important matters, it was evident, that they were all being viewed through the prism of India-US relations.

When President Bush visited New Delhi in March 2006, he and Prime Minister Manmohan Singh "expressed satisfaction with the great progress the US and India have made in advancing our strategic partnership to meet the global challenges of the 21st century. The successful transformation of the US-India relationship will have a decisive and positive influence on the future international system as it evolves in the new century." Placing the nuclear deal squarely within the framework of the "progress made in deepening the global partnership between the US and India since their joint statement of July 18, 2005," the President and Prime Minister reaffirmed their "commitment to expand even further the growing ties between these two countries." It was against this background that they "welcomed the successful completion of the separation plan" and looked forward "to the full implementation of the commitments in the July 18, 2005 agreement."

PRIME MINISTER'S STATEMENT TO PARLIAMENT

Prime Minister Manmohan Singh made a statement in the Lok Sabha on March 7, 2006 on the visit of the US President in which he claimed that "the Separation Plan that is being outlined is not only consistent with the imperatives of our national security, it also protects our vital research and development interests."

President Bush acted on his promise to ask the US Congress to take steps for necessary legislation for Indo-US nuclear cooperation. On July 27 the US Congress passed the Bill amending the Atomic Energy Act of 1954 making special provisions for India. Earlier, on June 29 the Senate Foreign Relations Committee had given approval to the Senate version of the Bill. There were some differences in certain provisions in the two

Bills and it was explained they would be reconciled in the final Act.

There was widespread criticism in India of the two Bills which contained many provisions which were against the interests of India, especially in the areas of foreign policy and strategic autonomy.

In replying to the discussion in Rajya Sabha on Civil Nuclear Energy Cooperation with the United States on August 17, 2006, the Prime Minister admitted that "we have concerns over both the House and Senate versions of the Bill." On the criticism that "we have compromised our foreign policy," the Prime Minister said, "We are unswerving in our commitment to an independent foreign policy. . . . I would again reiterate that the proposed US legislation on India would not be allowed to become an instrument to compromise India's sovereignty."

Referring to the key provisions in the US Bills to which references were made in the debate in the Parliament he identified nine more points and gave the following assurances to the Parliament:

(*i*) On full civil nuclear cooperation: "We will not allow any dilution that would prevent us from securing the full benefits of civil nuclear cooperation."
(*ii*) On principle of reciprocity: "I had earlier assured the House that reciprocity is the key to our understanding of the implementation of the July 2005 Statement. . . . Our position is that we will accept only IAEA safeguards on the nuclear facilities, in a phased manner and as identified in the Separation Plan only when all nuclear restrictions on India have been lifted."
(*iii*) On certification: "The draft Senate Bill requires the US President to make an annual report to the Congress that includes certification that India is in full compliance of its non-proliferation and other commitments. We have made it [*sic*] clear to the USA our opposition to these provisions as being contrary to the letter and spirit of July Statement."

(*iv*) On India as a State Possessing Advanced Nuclear Technology: "We have made it clear to the US that India's strategic programme is totally outside the purview of the July Statement and we oppose any legislative provisions that mandate scrutiny of either our nuclear weapons programme or our unsafeguarded nuclear facilities."

(*v*) On Safeguards Agreements and Fuel Assurances: "We will not allow any verification measures regarding our safeguarded nuclear facilities beyond those contained in an India-Specific Safeguards Agreement with the IAEA. Therefore there is no question of allowing American inspectors to roam around our nuclear facilities."

(*vi*) On integrity and reliability of our strategic programme: "In my statement of March 7, 2006 I had assured the Parliament that the Separation Plan would not adversely affect our strategic programme. We will not allow external scrutiny of our strategic programme in any manner, much less allow it to be a condition for future nuclear cooperation between India and the international community."

(*vii*) On moratorium on the production of fissile material: "Our position on the matter is unambiguous. We are not prepared to accept a moratorium on the production of fissile material."

(*viii*) On non-discriminatory global nuclear disarmament: "Our commitment towards non-discriminatory global disarmament remains."

(*ix*) On cessation of future cooperation: "There is provision in the proposed US law that were India to detonate a nuclear explosive device, the US will have the right to cease further cooperation. Our position on this is unambiguous. The US has been intimated that reference to nuclear detonation in the India-US Bilateral Nuclear Cooperation Agreement as a condition for future cooperation is not acceptable to us."[5]

A close examination of the statement shows that a distinction was made in the Prime Minister's explanation between the political and technical aspects of the deal. On the technical aspects he appeared to reflect the concerns expressed in Parliament and outside and was ready to give assurances. On foreign policy implications he was much less convincing, especially after the votes against Iran in September 2005 and February 2006 at the International Atomic Energy Agency (IAEA), obviously under pressure from the United States.

THE HYDE ACT

On December 9, 2006, the US legislation was finalized reconciling the two Bills from the Congress and Senate. President Bush signed on December 18 The Henry J. Hyde US-India Peaceful Nuclear Energy Cooperation Act 2006, named after the outgoing Chairman of the Senate Foreign Relations Committee. The Hyde Act provided the basis and framework on which the 123 agreement was struck. However, it retained most of the provisions which the Prime Minister had objected to during the Rajya Sabha debate. As Siddharth Varadarajan wrote,

> It is a measure of the American legislature's indifference to the assurances conveyed by the Prime Minister to the Indian Parliament on August 17 that most of the objections he raised about the legislative shape given to the US-India nuclear agreement have largely been ignored. Worse, the US Congress – with the encouragement and support of the Bush administration – has actually tried to mislead the Indian establishment and public opinion by introducing cosmetic or procedural changes that leave unchanged the shifting of goalposts that has consistently occurred since the two countries signed their joint statement in July last year.[6]

While the Prime Minister asserted in Parliament that India would not settle for anything less than "full civil energy cooperation," the Hyde Act made it clear that the US had no intention to allow India to access enrichment and reprocessing technologies.

On the issue of reciprocity, it was clear from the Hyde Act that there was very little of it, as the agreement could go to the Congress and restrictions lifted only after India signed safeguards agreement with the IAEA and clearance from the Nuclear Suppliers Group. The Prime Minister had claimed, "We will accept IAEA safeguards only when nuclear restrictions on India have been lifted."

The Prime Minister had used very strong language to oppose the provision about "certification." All that the Hyde Act did was to replace the word "certification" with "assessment." Thus the US President is still obligated by Section 104(g)(2) (1) to report every year his assessment of whether India is complying. He must also provide his assessment of whether India is working with the US to contain and constrain Iran.

The Prime Minister had said he would "oppose any legislative provisions that mandate the scrutiny of either our nuclear programmes or our unsafeguarded facilities." He said: "The Act mandates the US President to scrutinize in minute detail every aspect of our nuclear programme, including dual use capabilities and the production and import of nuclear facilities. Of course India is not obliged to facilitate this scrutiny, which arguably takes place even now."[7]

Contrary to the Prime Minister's assurance that the nuclear deal would involve the US helping to guarantee uninterrupted fuel supplies, the Act enjoins the US to oppose the stockpiling fuel beyond a small reserve to take care of market imperfections.

The Prime Minister insisted on maintaining the integrity and autonomy of India's civilian nuclear programme, and that it hinged on the right to reprocessing. On this matter the Hyde Act is silent.

The Prime Minister assured Parliament about India's commitment to non-discriminatory universal nuclear disarmament. But the Hyde Act seeks India's cooperation only against horizontal proliferation and only for South Asian nuclear disarmament.

The Prime Minister strongly objected to the "provision in the proposed US law that were India to explode a nuclear explosive device, the US will have the right to cease further cooperation." But interestingly the Prime Minister did not ask for a change in the provision, all that he asked for was that such a provision should not be included in the 123 agreement. Not having a reference to nuclear test in the 123 agreement but pretending to ignore the clear provision in the Hyde Act became one of the strategies through which the Indian government unconvincingly tried to escape from the onerous demands of the Hyde Act.

The Prime Minister had told Parliament in August 2006:

> I had taken up with President Bush our concerns regarding provisions in the two Bills. It is clear that if the final product is in the current form, India will have grave difficulties in accepting the bills. . . . If US legislation or NSG guidelines impose extraneous conditions on India, the Government will draw necessary conclusions consistent with my commitment to the Parliament.

After the passage of the Hyde Act, in his suo moto statement made to Parliament on December 12, 2006, External Affairs Minister Pranab Mukherji sought to assure the House that the US legislation fully reflects the Joint Statements of President Bush and Prime Minister Manmohan Singh on July 18, 2005 and March 2, 2006. He said in regard to the "principles and concerns that have guided our approach to the nuclear understanding the Prime Minister had set forth the Government's position when he spoke to the Parliament on August 17, 2006."

He added, "I would also like to share with the House that the Government has taken note of certain extraneous and prescriptive provisions in the legislation."[8] He did not specify what these provisions were but from the remarks that followed it was evident they referred to foreign policy and strategic programme.

The Hyde Act deserves close examination. As Rajiv Sikri pointed out,

> A reading of the Hyde Act brings out clearly Congressional thinking and motivation in passing the Hyde Act. The broad objectives of the Bush administration are no different, as confirmed by various officials of the US administration. Two principal US objectives stand out. The first, perhaps the most important, is to ensure that India's foreign policy is "congruent" to that of the USA, with this deal expected to "induce greater political and material support to the achievement of US goals." India's growing economic and political role in the world is seen as a "new and strategic opportunity to advance US goals." Iran gets a specific mention with the US expecting India's "full cooperation to dissuade, isolate and if necessary to sanction and contain Iran."[9]

POLITICAL DIMENSIONS

From the beginning New Delhi attempted to downplay or ignore the political dimensions of the deal. The July 2005 Joint Statement was the result of burgeoning strategic partnership between USA and India. It came as the follow up of India accepting the US conditions of "help" for making India become a major world power in the twenty-first century. The immediate background was a defence cooperation agreement entered into between Washington and New Delhi taking into account that the military ties between the two countries had reached "hitherto unimaginable and unprecedented levels of cooperation," just twenty days before the Joint Statement. The Joint Statement began with declaring the signatories' intention "to transform the relationship between their countries and establish a global partnership." It specifically "expressed satisfaction at the New Framework for the US-India Relationship as a basis for future cooperation."[10]

The Manmohan Singh government faithfully traversed the nuclear path charted by the BJP-led NDA government, endorsing every formal and informal undertaking that had been given to the Bush administration and adding a few new undertakings of its own. Manmohan Singh fully knew that in following the path to a nuclear deal with the USA, he was going down the road of the forfeiture of our strategic autonomy, which his predecessor had taken.

The other principal objective relates to non-proliferation, through strengthening and sustaining the implementation of the NPT. India remaining outside the NPT "poses a potential challenge to the goals of global non-proliferation," the Hyde Act says. A corollary objective is to curb India's nuclear weapon capability. In a semantic concession to the earlier Democratic mantra of "cap, rollback and eliminate" the objective now is to seek to "halt the increase in nuclear weapons arsenals in South Asia and promote their reduction and eventual elimination."

From the time the Hyde Act was passed, two contradictory lines were pursued by the Indian establishment. One was that some of the sections in the Act causing concern were non-binding. This claim was mainly based on the statement made by President Bush at the time of signing the law. We will examine the claim in some detail later. The other line was that the Hyde Act is a US law which does not apply to India at all and India will be bound only by the 123 agreement. This also will be examined later. Suffice it to point out at this stage that the Prime Minister in his statement to the Rajya Sabha mentioned "grave difficulties in *accepting the bills*" (emphasis added).

There is a fascinating but frustrating division of labour between senior officials in Washington and New Delhi about explanation on the implications of the nuclear deal. People in India have to listen to the officials in Washington to understand what is going on as the officials in New Delhi are reticent to the extent of denying information. In our capital they call this transparency. So it was up to Nicholas Burns, US Undersecretary of State, the chief architect of the accord on the US side, to explain in an article in the *Washington Post* the true nature of US-India relationship and the role of the nuclear deal in it. He said that "the pace of progress between Washington and Delhi has been so rapid and the potential benefit to American interests so substantial that I believe within a generation Americans may view India as one of the two or three most important strategic partners."[11] He put the nuclear agreement in perspective when he described it as "the symbolic and public centrepiece of the new partnership." He explained US objectives in the partnership with India. "Our first priority is to give governmental support to the huge growth in business between the Indian and American private sector. . . . Second, we can do much more to create a strategic military partnership. We need to build on an already series of joint military exercises to improve the interoperability of our armed forces to respond to global contingencies. We also aim to complete a series of defence sales that meet India's needs and complement our overall defence relationship. . . . Finally I am confident the US and India can work closely together on the key foreign policy challenges in South Asia," Burns said. "One of the main challenges is to isolate Iran." And then he said that something that most Indians were not probably aware of: "We are working together to try to stop the increasingly bloody civil war in Sri Lanka and bring stability and real democracy to Nepal and Bangladesh."[12]

This explanation from the chief US architect of the India-US nuclear deal was enough to dispel doubts about the nature of the deal. The deal is "the symbolic and the public centrepiece" of military alliance and economic collaboration. He made it abundantly clear that the deal was not primarily about nuclear energy. The first priority was on the economic front and primarily in the interests of US corporations in India. Siddharth Varadarajan wrote, "For all the controversy that nuclear negotiations between India and the United States have generated from July 2005, there is one point on which the supporters and opponents of the deal in both countries tend to agree wholeheartedly: the nuclear agreement is not about energy."[13]

THE 123 AGREEMENT

On July 27, Minister of External Affairs Pranab Mukherji and Secretary of State Condoleezza Rice issued a joint statement announcing the completion of negotiations with the 123 Agreement calling this a "historic milestone in the strategic partnership between India and the USA." On the same day both in New Delhi and in Washington top officials presented to the media some details of the Agreement – not the text of the Agreement – in separate fact-sheets. The subtle but identifiable differences in the fact-sheets and the visible distinction in presentation in the two capitals not only reflected two marketing strategies to the general public of the two countries but also the relative emphasis each government gave to pertinent issues in the Agreement. They provided an indication not only of the differences in expectations on the deal in the two capitals but possible differences in interpretation of key provisions and even official anxieties.

The Indian side led by M.K. Narayanan, National Security Adviser and including Shiv Shankar Menon, Foreign Secretary, and Anil Kakodkar, Chairman of the Atomic Energy Commission, attempted to present a sanitized version of the Agreement, projecting the impression that it was a stand-alone agreement on nuclear energy pure and simple and having nothing to do with anything else. The Agreement has neither any external basis nor any implications, they claimed. When asked about what the Americans were getting out of the deal in terms of arms deals, Narayanan said there were no references to arms deals in any of the negotiations. The Foreign Secretary was emphatic, "There were no conditions. This is an agreement on energy. We did not negotiate anything else."

In presenting the Washington version of the fact-sheet Nicholas Burns candidly put the Agreement in context. He called it historic and said "it has already become the symbolic centerpiece of a growing global partnership between the two countries," echoing his *Washington Post* article. In his prepared opening statement he said, "I think now that we have consummated the civil nuclear deal between us, if we look down the road in the future, we are going to see far greater defence cooperation between the USA and India: training, exercises, we hope defence sale of American military technology to the Indian armed forces, greater means of global cooperation." Replying to questions, he said India is entering into a closer military relationship with the US. "And as I said in my prepared statement, I think that is going to be one of the very significant horizons of this partnership."[14]

Some of the differences in the fact-sheets may be pointed out. The Indian fact-sheet only noted that 123 Agreement "provides for the application of IAEA safeguards to transferred material and equipment." The US fact-sheet, on the other hand, emphasizes that the 123 Agreement commits India to safeguards in perpetuity.

As for Nuclear Supply Group, the Indian fact-sheet said that the Group's guidelines must be changed to enable the NSG to trade with India "as an equal partner." The US fact sheet, on the other hand, only said that the NSG should make an India-specific exception to the full scope safeguards requirement but did not speak of India being treated as an equal partner.

There was a significant and probably deliberate omission in the Indian fact-sheet. Neither in the enumeration of the next steps nor anywhere else was the reference to the need for the US Congress to approve the 123 Agreement. The American fact-sheet clearly stated this.

The text of the Indo-US nuclear cooperation agreement, also known as 123 Agreement, was released on August 3. In 22 pages the 17 articles of the Agreement are a product of not only elaborate negotiations but also skilful drafting papering over differences with cosmetic changes. A studious attempt has been made to give the impression that it is a self-contained document.

The Bharatiya Janata Party on August 4 came out with a statement saying it was "unable to accept" the 123 Agreement on India-USA civil nuclear cooperation as finalized and "would definitely seek a review of the agreement when it comes to power" as it was of the view that it constituted "an assault on the nuclear sovereignty and foreign policy of India." It demanded the appointment of a joint parliamentary committee to examine the agreement in detail. The BJP would like the Constitution to be amended to bind all future governments and ensure that all agreements that affect the country's sovereignty, territorial integrity and national security shall be ratified by Parliament. The party was concerned about the Agreement's implications for India's strategic programme and independent foreign policy.[15]

The BJP's objections were, one, the implementation of the agreement would be governed by national laws of the two countries, hence the provisions of the Hyde Act applied. Two, reference to "aspects of the associated nuclear cycle" implied that the agreement did not cover the full nuclear cycle; provision for transfer of sensitive nuclear technology, heavy water production technology and major critical components should have been covered by the agreement but had not been covered; the US right of end-use verification could mean American inspectors freely roaming India's nuclear installations (a fear that was discounted by the Prime Minister in Parliament on August 17, 2006).

While several of the objections the BJP raised appeared to be valid, there was a fatal flaw in the stance of the party. It was the BJP-led government which initiated the nuclear dialogue with Washington in the first place, and they almost came to an agreement with the USA. The paradigm shift in India's foreign policy arose literally out of the nuclear weapon programme of the Vajpayee government which opted for a military alliance with the Bush administration in the wake of the War on Terror. It was actually the BJP-led government's unbridled support to the National Missile Defence of the USA that led to the surrender of India's strategic autonomy.[16]

THE LEFT POSITION AND THE PM'S RESPONSE

A principled, well thought-out and cogent position on the 123 agreement was spelt out by the Left parties on August 7 in a joint statement by the leaders of the CPI (M), CPI, RSP and Forward Bloc:[17]

> The Left parties have consistently held that the nuclear cooperation agreement should not be seen in isolation from

> the overall strategic ties with the United States. It is therefore not possible to view the text of the bilateral agreement negotiated with the United States as separate and compartmentalized without considering its implications for India's foreign policy strategic autonomy and the repercussions of the US quest to make India its reliable ally in Asia.

The statement pointed out that the bilateral agreement could not be seen outside the Hyde Act and that serious concern had been expressed by the Left parties about various conditions inserted into the Act by the US Congress. It particularly noted the provisions of the Act which have direct reference to India's foreign policy. The stipulations in the Hyde Act were against India's position on nuclear disarmament. The statement said, "While the 123 agreement is presented as a victory for India's positions and conforming to the Prime Minister's assurances in the Parliament, there are a number of issues on which it falls short of what the Prime Minister had assured the Parliament." The statement pointed out that "the bilateral nuclear agreement should be seen as a crucial step to lock in India into the US global strategic design. Alongside negotiations on the accord, steps have been taken for closer military cooperation."

The Left parties called upon the government "not to proceed with the operationalizing of the agreement" without a review of the strategic aspects of Indo-US relations in Parliament. They would press for a constitutional amendment for bringing treaties and certain bilateral agreements before parliament for approval.

The Prime Minister made a statement in the Lok Sabha on August 13, 2007 on Civil Nuclear Energy Cooperation Agreement with the United States claiming that the pledge "that the Government will make every effort so that the vision of the Joint Statements of July 2005 and March 2006 becomes a living reality" had been redeemed.[18]

The main points he made in the statement were the following:

(*i*) The concept of full civil nuclear cooperation has been clearly underlined in this Agreement. A significant aspect of the Agreement is our right to reprocess US origin spent fuel. This has been secured upfront.
(*ii*) The principle of reciprocity which was integral to the July 2005 Statement has been fully safeguarded in this Agreement.
(*iii*) This Agreement further confirms that US cooperation with India is a permanent one. There is no provision that states that US cooperation with India will be subject to an annual certification.
(*iv*) As agreed in the March separation plan India has only accepted safeguards that will be reflected in an India-specific Safeguards Agreement with the IAEA. We have not consented to any provision that mandates scrutiny of our nuclear weapon programme or any unsafeguarded facilities.
(*v*) The Agreement gives assurance of uninterrupted fuel supply. An important assurance given is the commitment of support for India's effort to build up strategic reserves of nuclear fuel to meet the lifetime requirements of India's reactors.
(*vi*) The Agreement does not in any way impact on India's ability to produce and use fissile material for its current and future strategic needs.
(*vii*) The Agreement does not in any way affect India's right to undertake future nuclear tests, if it is necessary in India's national interests. A decision to undertake a future nuclear test would be India's sovereign decision, one that rests solely with the Government.[19]

Stating that "India stands on the world stage as an influential and respected member of the international community" and claiming that "there is independence in our thoughts and independence in our actions," the Prime Minister said "there is no question that we will ever compromise, in any manner our independent foreign policy. We shall retain our strategic autonomy."

The Prime Minister paid glowing tributes to President Bush for making the Agreement possible: "The strengthening and enhancement of our bilateral relations is an objective that has received his unstinting support and commitment." The Prime Minister's statement reflected the calculated attempt on the part of the government to project the 123 Agreement as a self-contained document not bound by any US law and with no conditions, implications or consequences other than those mentioned in the Agreement.

In taking this position the Prime Minister withheld from parliament two important factors. One, that this Agreement has to be accepted by the US Congress and that it is subject to the provisions of the Hyde Act. Two, in the Joint Statement of July 2005 the nuclear deal is placed within the context of US-India strategic cooperation and is directly linked to the Defence Cooperation Agreement of June 2005.

It is the right to reprocess spent fuel that was highlighted by the Prime Minister as the most important gain for India. It is true that this right is essential for the nuclear programme and that it has been conceded only in the last stage of the negotiations. But the Prime Minister's claim that "it has been secured upfront" is not correct. Under Article 6(iii) the US grants India "consent to reprocess." It is pointed out that the fact-sheet of the Ministry of External Affairs had used the expression "prior consent" but "prior" does not find a place in the text of the Agreement. To exercise this right, India has to maintain a dedicated facility for reprocessing under IAEA safeguards. There is also reference to "such other provisions as may be agreed by the parties" indicating possible additional conditions by the US causing uncertainty about reprocessing. The text of the Agreement clearly shows the US has granted India the right to reprocess only in principle. The grant of actual right may take many years with the US retaining a veto on Indian reprocessing till then.

The Prime Minister's claim about "full cooperation" also is only partially valid. The Agreement does not allow India to access reprocessing enrichment or heavy water technologies or components or for dual use components in reprocessing, enrichment or heavy water facilities. Article 5.2 only says an amendment to the Agreement is needed to allow such transfers.

The Prime Minister knew such an amendment was unlikely. The claim about reciprocity is perhaps even less valid, especially when the Prime Minister refers to the 2005 July Joint Statement. The changing of goal posts unilaterally by the US, imposing new conditions and not taking reciprocal actions has seriously impaired the principle of reciprocity. The Prime Minister's claim that only IAEA inspectors will be allowed into our nuclear facilities has to be seen along with some provisions in the Agreement which suggest a different intent and call into question the Prime Minister's statement in the Parliament that "there is no question of American inspectors roaming around Indian nuclear facilities." It has been pointed out, "There is an unusual clause in the agreement which speaks of India facilitating the entry of experts 'when execution of an agreement or contract pursuant to the agreement' requires this. This clause does not figure in the 123 agreements the US has signed with other Non-Nuclear Weapon States (NNWS) such as Japan and Morocco and is perhaps intended to smooth the way for US end-use verification efforts, should they become ever necessary following an IAEA determination on the non-application of safeguards."[20]

The Prime Minister stated that there is no provision that states that the US cooperation with India will be subject to an annual certification process. The Prime Minister is correct, but up to a point; there is no such provision in the 123 Agreement. The "annual certification process" was unacceptable to India, the Prime Minister had told the Parliament an year ago. As we have seen, the Hyde Act uses the term "assessment" instead of "certification" without changing the procedure of annual report by the President. Did the Prime Minister really mean that since such a provision is not in the Agreement, the US President and the Congress can dispense with such procedure? And why did the Prime Minister use the word "certification" which is not in the Hyde Act?

In the statement the Prime Minister reiterates India's well-known position on nuclear disarmament. As we have seen, however, the Hyde Act envisages India's cooperation in the arms control agenda of the United States, not for non-discriminatory universal disarmament for which India has always stood. The Prime Minister was emphatic in asserting that "This Agreement does not in any way affect India's right to undertake future nuclear tests. A decision to undertake a nuclear test would be our sovereign decision." The Prime Minister is on very firm ground in stating this. Nobody can question India's sovereign right to test. But the Prime Minister did not say what happens with regard to the Agreement if India conducts a test. Under its law the US will impose sanctions. Under the Hyde Act the US will terminate the 123 Agreement. India has the sovereign right to test and the US has its national laws to act.

In fact it may be good that India never again conducts a nuclear test. But that is not the issue. The issue is that not conducting a test has been made a condition precedent to the Agreement. One of the most unambiguously worded provisions of the Hyde Act is that all commitments that may be entered upon as part of the framework of full civilian nuclear energy cooperation "shall cease to be effective if the President determines that India has detonated a nuclear explosive device." There is an indirect reference to India's future nuclear test in the Agreement. Article 14.2 says the US agrees to "take into account that may lead to termination or cessation resulted from [India's] serious concern about a changed security environment or as a response to similar actions by other States which could impact national security."

Brahma Chellany, strategic affairs expert, points out that "the United States besides upholding the primacy of its laws has gained two absolute rights, the right to unilaterally terminate cooperation with India at will (without arranging alternate supplies) and the right to take back all supplied items and materials."[21]

It confers on the US an unfettered and unfringeable right to terminate cooperation with India at will. Article 14.2 states, "The party seeking termination has the right to cease further cooperation under the agreement if it determines that a mutually acceptable resolution of outstanding issues has not been possible or cannot be achieved through consultation." That would put India at the mercy of the supplier, holding all the leverage. Even though termination is to take effect at the end of one-year period, the Agreement explicitly empowers the US to forthwith suspend all cooperation without much ado. The only requirement is that a "party giving notice of termination shall provide the reason for seeking such termination."

We may once again look in some detail at the place of the Hyde Act in the scheme of the nuclear deal. Once the Hyde Act was signed by President Bush, the government of India began taking the view that it could live with it as what was important was the 123 agreement to be negotiated. The line taken was that 123 agreement would take care of all the concerns of India, ignoring or deliberately hiding the fact that the basis for the bilateral agreement was the Hyde Act. Once the 123 agreement was concluded it was presented first by the officials and then by the Prime Minister that the Hyde Act was a US law and it was not applicable to India.

This was wrong and totally misleading but was part of a deliberate strategy. The strategy backfired and the government had later to admit the relevance of the Hyde Act.

The Hyde Act – the United States India Peaceful Atomic Energy Cooperation Act – is an India-specific legislation. There are no special legislations like this for the many 123 agreements the US has made with other countries. They all are directly linked to the Atomic Energy Act of the USA of 1954. But in the case of India it is the Hyde Act which provides the legal framework for the bilateral agreement. The Act provides the basis in US law for the 123 agreement between USA and India. A noticeable aspect in an otherwise elaborate document set out in meticulous detail is that there is no mention of the basis of its authority being derived from Section 123 of the US Atomic energy Act of 1954. This can be explained. There is a special law for

India. The Agreement has to be read with the mandatory provisions of the Henry Hyde Act which is the umbrella legislation in this case. The primacy of the Hyde Act which defines India specific terms and conditions over 41 pages is affirmed.

According to Undersecretary Nicholas Burns, "We kept reminding the Indian side and they were good enough to negotiate on the basis that anything we did had to fall within and respect the legal guidelines that the Congress had set forth." The 123 Agreement expressly reaffirms the Hyde Act by citing the applicability of national laws to govern nuclear energy cooperation between USA and India. Contrast that with what Parliament was told in December 2006 after the Hyde Act enactment. The government "has taken note of certain extraneous and prescriptive provisions which continue to be a concern and we will need to discuss them with the US administration before the bilateral cooperation agreement can be finalized." What was the result of such discussions, if any? Why was the government concerned about provisions in the Hyde Act if India was not bound by it? Why did the Prime Minister forcefully express concerns about the Bills of the Congress and the Senate if the legislation was not going to affect India? What was the need for all the assurances that the Prime Minister gave to the Parliament if the US legislation would have nothing to do with India?

We may recall what the Prime Minister told the Parliament in August 2006: "It is clear that if the final product is in the current form, India will have great difficulties in accepting the bills. . . . If US legislation or NSG guidelines impose extraneous conditions on India, the government will draw the necessary conclusions consistent with my commitment to the Parliament." So the bills, i.e. the Act out of them, *had to be acceptable to India*. As we have seen, most of the objectionable provisions were kept in the Act. By the Prime Minister's own reasoning the Hyde Act is unacceptable to India. Again the Government admitted that the legislation imposed extraneous conditions. Did the Government draw the necessary conclusions consistent with the Prime Minister's assurances? Obviously not.

The External Affairs Minister repeated in Parliament on August 17 that India was not bound by the Hyde Act. The Act, he said, was unacceptable as it contained "certain extraneous and prescriptive provisions" – the standard expression used by the Government from the time the Act was passed. "Whatever is said in the Hyde Act is not binding on us. How they deal with this is their problem." He appeared to silence the critics by quoting the statement of President Bush on signing the Act. It is of course true that the minister was quoting the President verbatim, but not in full. This is what the President actually said:

> Section 103 of the Act purports to establish the US policy with respect to various international affairs. My approval of the Act does not constitute any adoption of the statement of policy as US foreign policy. Given the Constitution's commitment to the Presidency of the authority to conduct the nation's foreign affairs, the executive branch shall construe such policy statements as advisory. Also if section 104(d)(2) of the Act were construed to prohibit the executive branch from transferring or approving the transfer of an item to India contrary to Nuclear Suppliers Group transfer guidelines that may be in effect at the time of such future transfer, a serious question would exist whether the provision unconstitutionally delegated power to an international body. In order to avoid this constitutional question, the executive branch will construe this section as advisory. . . . The executive branch will give sections 103 and 194(d)(2) the due weight that comity between the legislative and executive branches should require to the extent consistent with US foreign policy.[22]

The External Affairs Minister quoted this statement to buttress his argument that Hyde Act was not binding on India. Some annotation is clearly required here. To begin with, the Act was made by the US legislature to govern India-US relations on atomic energy. US cooperation with India on peaceful nuclear energy is bound by the Act. Any agreement made between the two countries on nuclear energy is bound by it. Therefore the 123 Agreement is bound by the Hyde Act. Further, the President's statement only says that his administration will construe one section and one subsection as advisory. The word non-binding is not used. Even while construing them as advisory, the President will give due weight to the position of the Congress. Moreover, the particular interpretations given by the present President are in no way binding on a future US President. Prime Minister Manmohan Singh had conceded in Parliament that "certain provisions, even if they are projected as non-binding, are contrary to the letter and spirit of the July 18, 2005 Joint Statement and that non-binding provisions have 'a certain weight' in the implementation of the legislation as a whole."

With regard to the provisions in the Hyde Act, the Left parties in their joint statement pointed out that "a number of these pertain to areas outside nuclear cooperation and are attempts to coerce India to accept the strategic goals of the US." These issues are:

1. Annual certification (assessment) and reporting to the Congress by the US President on a variety of foreign policy issues such as Indian foreign policy being congruent to that of the United States and more specifically India joining the efforts of isolating and even sanctioning Iran.
2. Indian participation and formal declaration of support for the US's highly controversial Proliferation Security Initiative, including the illegal policy of interdiction of vessels in international waters.
3. India conforming to various bilateral and multilateral agreements to which India is currently not a signatory, such as the US Missile Technology Control Regime, the Australia Group, etc.[23]

The statement further pointed out that "All these are part of the Hyde Act. The 123 Agreement refers only to the narrow question of supply of nuclear materials and cooperation on nuclear matters. The provisions of the Hyde Act are far wider than the 123 Agreement and could be used to terminate the 123 Agreement not only in the eventuality of a nuclear test but also for India not conforming to the US foreign policy."

As the Left parties intensified their opposition to the strategic tie-up with the US, the ruling United Progressive Alliance (UPA), which had earlier taken the position that the Hyde Act was of no relevance, attempted to defuse the political crisis by setting up a committee to look into the Left objections. The following statement was made by the External Affairs Minister Pranab Mukherji after a meeting of the leaders of the Congress and Left Parties. "In view of certain objections raised by the Left parties on the Indo-US bilateral agreement on nuclear cooperation, it has been decided to constitute a committee to go into these issues. The committee will look into certain aspects of the bilateral agreement, the implications of the Hyde Act on the 123 Agreement and self-reliance in the nuclear sector; the implications of the nuclear agreement on foreign policy and security cooperation. The committee will examine these issues. The operationalization of the deal will take into account the committee's findings."[24] However, this appears to be a tactical move by the UPA, with no firm commitment not to operationalize the deal.

WIDER IMPLICATIONS

In the coming months and perhaps even years we will have to live with the consequences of the differing interpretations of the nuclear agreement. As Michael Krepon and Alex Stolar point out, "The down-side risks of this deal are now becoming clearer, and will become even more evident by parsing the tortured language of the 123 Agreement. The governments of Manmohan Singh and George W. Bush appear to be interpreting key provisions of the agreement very differently, which can cause only more ill will and headaches in the future."[25]

Some of the wider implications of the strategic alliance between India and the USA deserve examination at this stage. There is enough evidence to show that the deal was shaped at a time when the US was focusing its attention on China. The apparent emergence of a quadrilateral alignment among the US, Japan, India and Australia has given rise to understandable concern in Beijing. Days before the first official-level consultation among these countries held in May 2007 on the sidelines of the Asia Regional Forum in Manila, China issued demarches to each participant seeking to know the purpose behind the meeting.

The Prime Minister sought to allay Chinese apprehensions by saying, "I have told Chinese President Hu Jintao that there is no question of ganging up against China" and added that the group is not a military alliance. Probably Indian officials thought that meeting on the sidelines of the ARF, the message would go out that the quadrilateral is essentially an adjunct to ARF, without perhaps realizing that any alliance between the US, Japan and India will not be seen in Beijing as related to ARF or ASEAN. Beijing knows only too well that the US has been engaged in seeking to hold a patchwork of military and strategic alliances around China and that in Washington's scheme India has been assigned a role in the containment of China. Indian leaders seem to be confident that they can handle problems with China even while deepening strategic and military relationship with the USA. But they cannot afford to ignore Washington's calculations about India's role.

The new quadrilateral alignment made a dramatic entry into the scene by joint military and naval exercises in the Bay of Bengal in early September 2007.

As we have seen, the India-US defence agreement of June 28, 2005 is closely linked to the nuclear deal and that assumes special significance in the light of Nicholas Burns' statement on the 123 agreement. *People's Daily online* of July 7, 2005 commented that "when cries grow louder in the US political circles for the construction of an Asian allies' network to guard against China, the US Defence Secretary signed his visiting Indian counterpart an eye-catching defence cooperation agreement" and that "it regarded as another important step Washington made in

Asia which is partly intended to diminish China's influence in the region and expand US strategic interests in Asia." It added, "Although both sides say the agreement has nothing to do with China, the China factor is only too obvious."

The broad sweep of US strategy in Asia-Pacific was spelled out in Pentagon's policy assessment *Quadrennial Defence Review* published in February 2006. "The country will attempt to dissuade any military competition from developing disruptive or other capabilities that could enable regional hegemony or hostile action against the US," the document says. It then identifies China as the most likely and dangerous competitor of the sort. Of the major and emerging powers China has the greatest potential to compete militarily with the US and field military technologies that could over time offset traditional US military advantages – absent US counterstrategies.[26]

Michael Klare wrote:

> Slowly but surely, the grand strategy of the Bush administration is being revealed. It is not aimed primarily at the defeat of global terrorism, the incapacitation of rogue states or the spread of democracy in the Middle East. The truly commanding objective and the underlying basis for budgetary and troop deployment is the containment of China. Despite President's Bush's preoccupation with Iraq and Iran, the White House is reemphasizing a paramount focus on China fuelling a new arms race and spreading militarism in Asia with devastating consequences.[27]

China was distinctly on the backburner post-September 11, but it is clear that from mid-2005 Washington is clearly focusing on China. The military expansion of China as well as the diplomatic and economic advances it has made not only in the Asian region but also in Africa and Latin America has projected new dimensions of the Chinese challenge. There is enough evidence to believe that the Bush administration is clearly engaged in a concerted and calculated effort to contain Chinese power and influence. Klare points out that "This effort appears to have three objectives – to cement existing relations with Japan, Australia and Korea into a robust anti-China alliance system to bring other nations especially India into the system and to expand US military capabilities in the Asian region." Klare added that an even bigger prize in Washington's view would be the "integration of India into this emerging alliance system,"[28] a possibility first suggested in an article in *Foreign Affairs* by Rice before the first election of George W. Bush as President.[29] In a way Rice followed up this suggestion in her remarks at the Sophia University in March 2005. There Rice equated US-India relationship with the US-Japan and US-Korea relationships.

It is significant to note that for the first time, the joint statement of the US-Japan Security Consultative Committee (the annual meeting of the Defence and Foreign Ministers of the two countries), sets out as "a common strategic objective the task of continuing to build upon partnership with India to advance areas of common interests and increase cooperation recognizing that India's continued growth is increasingly tied to the prosperity, freedom and security of the region."[30]

While President Bush did not allude to the administration's Chinese agenda in making the nuclear deal with India, saying only that it would "lay foundation for a durable defence relationship," many observers saw a China factor in the relationship. The strategic relationship of the US with Japan is to ensure it has a close and capable ally on China's southeastern flank. The deal with India reflects, these observers believe, a plan to build an alliance on China's southwestern flank. According to Steven R. Weisman, more US lawmakers view the nuclear deal as an expression of the administration's desire to convert India into a "counterweight to China." He added that the "the goal of making India an ally outweighs concerns over the risks of spreading nuclear skills or bomb-making materials."[31] Paul Richter commented, "A key factor behind the nuclear cooperation between the USA and India was a single tradeoff. The White House was willing to risk losing ground in the world wide campaign to limit the spread of nuclear weapons for a deal with India that could help it counter the rising power of China."[32] The Hyde Act makes it clear that Washington wants to ensure Indian foreign policy to be congruent to America's and expects to induce greater political and material support for the advancement of American goals. No doubt one of the main goals of America is the containment of China.

The linkage between the nuclear deal and the "Global Democracy Initiative" has to be underlined. The famous Joint Statement of July 2005 which gave shape to the deal said: "Develop and support through the new US-India Global Democracy Initiative in countries that seek such assistance, institutions, and resources that strengthen the foundations that make democracies credible and effective."

A new stage of the US thrust on global democracy began at the end of 2003 when President Bush virtually named the target countries for spreading democracy. Speaking at a National Endowment for Democracy function he remarked that the US commitment to democracy is being tested in countries like Cuba, Burma, North Korea, Zimbabwe and China as well as the Middle East. Bush reiterated the theme in his second inaugural address (January 20, 2005) by announcing a US policy of seeking and supporting "the growth of democratic movements and institutions in every nature and culture with the ultimate goal of ending tyranny in the world."

Manmohan Singh's speech at the banquet given by President Bush in his honour in Washington was an abject endorsement of the American political orientation which fully reflected the neo-con agenda. He said, "We must strengthen democratic capacities jointly. We must oppose the evil of terrorism together. To meet such challenges we must be on the same page. We must speak the same language and display the same resolve."

When President Bush came to New Delhi in early March 2006 for the next stage of the nuclear deal, at the only public occasion, the speech at the Purana Qila, again the theme for was "global democracy":

> The world has benefited from the example of Indian democracy and now the world needs India's leadership in freedom's cause. As a global power India has a historic duty to support democracy around the world. India's leadership is needed in a world that is hungry for freedom. Men and women from North Korea to Burma to Syria to Zimbabwe to Cuba yearn for their liberty. In Iran, a proud people is held hostage by a small elite that denies basic liberties, sponsors terrorism and pursues nuclear weapons. We must stand with reformers and dissidents and civil society organizations and hasten the day when the people of these nations can determine their own future and choose their own leaders.[33]

In simple terms, what Bush asked for was regime change in a number of countries, including some with whom India has the friendliest relations. He wanted India to work with "reformers and dissidents" in these countries and change their leaders i.e. regimes. Bush was reminding Manmohan Singh about the support he had pledged for this neo-con agenda.

"The Bush administration is inclined toward historic game-changing, geo-strategic initiatives. The proposed US-India deal certainly fits this mould."[34] Therefore it is important to challenge any presentation of this project in isolation and as self-contained and stand-alone. The wider picture of the nuclear deal, in which one can clearly see the many strategic implications and political dimensions, has to be kept upfront. CPI (M) General Secretary Prakash Karat said: "The nuclear deal, the military agreement and the economic polices designed to advance the interests of US capital are part of the trio which are harmful for India's sovereignty, independent foreign policy and people's economic interests."[35]

M.K. Bhadrakumar

India, Central Asia and the Great Game

The high-ranking officials of the United States have been explicit that they place the civil nuclear cooperation with India within the broad framework of a "strategic partnership" with India. There is no denying, in other words, that our so-called "nuclear deal" has wider implications for India's security and foreign policy for decades to come. Senior US officials have stressed the role of India as a "strategic partner" in East Asia. Translated in plain terms, Washington expects India to play a role in augmenting its policy of "containment" of Russia and China. This American expectation is logical and is a critical component of the US global strategy insofar as the US's Cold War era "containment" policy against Russia and China cannot and will not work so long as there is a "multipolar" world order, and India remains an autonomous player on the Asian continent pursuing an independent foreign policy. Many features of the 123 Agreement and the Hyde Act are patently geared to lock Indian policies into the US regional and global strategies for the next few decades. Viewing them in isolation or underplaying their danger to the country's sovereignty will be a grave mistake. Unfortunately, the United

Progressive Alliance (UPA) government has resorted to sophistry in misguiding the public opinion so as to somehow rush the 123 Agreement through.

Indeed, serious aberrations have already begun appearing in the country's independent foreign policy. The vote against Iran at the International Atomic Energy Agency (IAEA) in 2005; the calibrated distancing from the Palestinian cause; the neglect of the traditional ties of friendship with Russia; the military cooperation agreements with the US; the increasing frequency of the visits of US warships to Indian sea ports – all these point towards a complete reorientation of India's foreign policy. Now it is clear that the government is pressing ahead with the entire range of the agenda of the previous National Democratic Alliance (NDA) government known as the Next Stage in Strategic Partnership (NSSP), which envisaged that India and the US would be "natural allies" in the 21st century. The Malabar Exercises in the Bay of Bengal in September 2007 underscore beyond doubt that the US stratagem to co-opt India into its Asian agenda is already far advanced and that the government in Delhi is willingly allowing itself to be drawn into a quadripartite alliance with the US, Japan and Australia. To be sure, such an alliance suits the US interests and strategy. But what is there in it for India?

Not surprisingly, the US is making an all-out effort to claw its way back into the Asian continent. American strategists realise the critical importance of Asia in the coming decades as the countries of this region are virtually emerging as the locomotives of the world economy. But the ground reality is that the US influence in Asia is diminishing. In Washington's estimation, the main challenge is somehow to divide Asia and thereby to "contain" China's expanding influence and Russia's resurgence. Central Asia is a major theatre where this Great Game is playing out. The history of the Indian subcontinent amply bears out that the geopolitics of Central Asia would inevitably impact on India's security and welfare. India would have an abiding interest in contributing to the stability and security of Central Asia. In the present context, this means that first and foremost India should cooperate and collaborate with Russia and China in the stabilization of Central Asia. The perfect vehicle for this purpose would be the Shanghai Cooperation Organization (SCO).

But the worrisome signs are that against the backdrop of the Indo-US nuclear deal and the larger framework of "strategic partnership" with the United States, India's autonomy and freedom to pursue a Central Asia policy in tune with our national interests is coming under strain.

SCO MARKS ITS PRESENCE

It may seem improbable that a regional cooperation organization commences its annual summit meeting against the backdrop of a military exercise. The European Union, Association of South East Asian Nations, Organization of African Unity, Organization of Latin American States – none of them has ever done that. Therefore, the Shanghai Cooperation Organization (SCO) indeed made a very big point by way of holding its large-scale military exercise on August 9-17, 2007. The SCO was loudly proclaiming to the international community that there was no "vacuum" in Central Asia's strategic space that needed to be filled in by security organizations from outside the region.

The exercise, codenamed "Peace Mission 2007" was held in Chelyabinsk in Russia's Volga-Ural military district and in Urumqi, capital of China's Xinjiang Autonomous Region. The SCO's annual summit meeting for 2007 took place in the Kyrgyz capital Bishkek on August 16. Following the summit, in a highly symbolic gesture, the heads of states and defence ministers of all SCO members – China, Russia, Kazakhstan, Kyrgyzstan, Uzbekistan and Tajikistan – watched the conclusion of the joint military exercise. The SCO has never held a full-scale military exercise involving all its member states. An estimated 6,500 troops took part in the exercise, including 2,000 Russian and 1,600 Chinese personnel. This was the first time that China deputed its airborne units for a military exercise abroad. Russia and China deployed 36 and 46 aircraft respectively and each contributed six IL-76 military transport aircraft to perform simulated airborne assaults.

A Chinese military expert, Peng Guangqian of China's Academy of Military Sciences, was quoted by *People's Daily* as saying, "The drill mainly aims to showcase the improved security cooperation among the SCO member states, the reinforced anti-terror capability of SCO members, the improved Sino-Russian relationship and the modernization of the member countries' armed forces." The government-owned *China Daily* underlined that the exercise showed "SCO cooperation over security has gone beyond the issues of regional disarmament and borders, for it includes how to deal with non-traditional threats such as terrorists, secessionist forces, and extremist religious groups." The Chinese Ministry of Defence in a statement stressed that the exercise "does not target other countries and does not involve interests of countries outside the SCO." Briefing the media, Russia's ground forces' deputy commander, General Vladimir Moltenskoi also said that the exercises were "not aimed at third countries."

CSTO EMBRACES CHINA

Despite these understatements, it was all too obvious that the Sino-Russian strategic cooperation was reaching a qualitatively new level. Russia and China quietly underscored this point shortly after the SCO drill by holding yet another anti-terrorist exercise – this time at the bilateral level – in the Moscow region on September 4-6, designated to promote inter-operability between their special forces. This public display of the growing security agenda in the Sino-Russian strategic partnership was codenamed "Cooperation 2007." The 3-day drill involved joint preparations and planning, combat deployments, and joint combat operations. China's elite "Snow Leopard Strike Force," which is reputed to be the most secretive Chinese special force, took part in the drill. This latest military exercise in September also involved the intelligence services of both Russia and China and it suggested unmistakably that the planning staffs of the two countries have factored the prospect of conducting an actual joint operation if a need arises.

However, the most important indicator in this direction is that a formal protocol of cooperation may soon be finalized between the SCO and the Collective Security Treaty Organization (CSTO). The document is expected to clearly define the cooperation trends between the two regional security organizations in the coming period. This is undoubtedly a major development on the Eurasian strategic space. The proposed formal link-up between CSTO and SCO in essence involves CSTO plus China, as the SCO member countries other than China are already members of the CSTO. (The CSTO member countries are Russia, Belarus, Armenia, Kazakhstan, Kyrgyztsan, Uzbekistan and Tajikistan.)

It cannot be lost on anyone that the CSTO-SCO partnership is being formalized soon after Moscow's decision on July 14 to suspend its participation in the Treaty on Conventional Armed Forces in Europe (CFE). The CFE was the first ever post-World War II conventional arms reduction treaty reached between the East and the West. The influential Russian strategic analyst Gleb Pavlovsky had warned on July 14, "Today's decision is not propaganda, it is a transition to a new serious phase in Russia's construction of a new security architecture against the background of the world's rearmament near on our borders." Referring to the relentless US encirclement of post-Soviet Russia, he added, "Virtually all countries along Russia's southern and western borders are being stuffed with missiles. . . . A mad arms race in the Caucasus, Caspian, and Black Sea regions is under way, and it is being maintained by European and non-European countries, none of them restricted by the CFE." In this context, Pavlovsky said, Moscow would opt preferably for "new contractual balances" in Europe and Asia. "If the countries of Europe and Asia are prepared for this, Russia will be the first to agree to such negotiations."

It is an interesting thought that we may be seeing in the CSTO-SCO institutional link-up the first evidence of these "new contractual balances." The Russian thinking in the direction of building up the CSTO's sinews as a counterweight to the North

Atlantic Treaty Organization (NATO) has been evident for some months. In December 2006, while addressing the CIS and Baltic States Media Forum, Deputy Prime Minister (concurrently Russia's defence minister at that time), Sergei Ivanov had said, "The next logical thing on the path of reinforcing international security may be to develop a cooperation mechanism between NATO and CSTO, *followed by a clear division of spheres of responsibility*. This approach offers the prospect of enabling us to possess sufficiently reliable and effective leverage for taking joint action in crisis situations in various regions of the world" (emphasis added).

It was not as if Ivanov was unaware that NATO was not in the least interested in dealings with the CSTO. (The CSTO countries cover roughly 70 per cent of the territory of the former Soviet Union.) For the past 3 years, Russia has been proposing the desirability of limited cooperation between CSTO and NATO in countering drug trafficking originating from Afghanistan. But NATO, at Washington's bidding, has been stalling. It has been NATO's (and Washington's) consistent policy not to recognize CSTO's *locus standi* as a regional security organization, and to instead deal with the CSTO member countries (Russia, Belarus, Kazakhstan, Uzbekistan, Kyrgyzstan, Tajikistan and Armenia) on a bilateral basis. Therefore, in actuality, shorn of *diplomatese*, what Ivanov was stressing was that Moscow would be every bit determined to resist NATO's encroachment into the territories of the former Soviet republics. This emanated out of Moscow's assessment that NATO wouldn't be averse to expanding even further, by offering membership to some CIS countries. Russia is opposed to such expansion, but its diplomatic efforts are not working. The military option has become necessary. In his speech, Ivanov not only made a resolute statement about the CSTO's place in Europe but also hinted that Moscow viewed the Central Asian countries in the SCO, especially China, as its potential bloc allies.

A few months later, in May 2007, while speaking at a conference in Bishkek on 21st century security threats and challenges, CSTO Secretary General Nikolai Bordyuzha frontally attacked NATO, saying it had been pursuing "a policy of projecting and consolidating its military-political presence in the Caucasus and in Central Asia." He added that these activities posed "challenges and risks" and undermined the stability in the post-Soviet space. Bordyuzha elaborated that the US's Central Asia strategy aimed at driving a "geopolitical wedge" between regional states on the one hand and Russia and the CSTO on the other. He said Washington's attempt was to re-orient the Central Asian states towards the US "in a new format, encompassing, besides the Central Asian states, Afghanistan, Pakistan, and in the future, India." Indeed, in the recent period, Russia has all but blunted NATO's Central Asia strategy. In retrospect, NATO overestimated its capacity to gatecrash into a region where Russia's traditional influence is overwhelming and where Russia is determined to keep things that way whatever it takes.

Over the past two years, Moscow has rapidly built up the CSTO as the bulwark against NATO in Central Asia. Some Russian commentators have forecast that the CSTO is destined to become a Warsaw Pact. Be that as it may, almost in direct proportion to Moscow's emphasis on the CSTO, there has been a rallying by the Central Asian countries under the CSTO, especially by Kazakhstan, which was a prime "target" identified by NATO in the region. Of course, Uzbekistan's return to the CSTO last year after nearly a decade's absence has significantly consolidated the reach of the organization over the Central Asian region.

SINO-RUSSIAN CONVERGENCE

Clearly, China appreciates that the contradictions and struggles between Russia and the Western powers in the post-cold war years are at a defining moment. Writing in the *People's Daily*, Wang Baofu, Deputy Director of the Institute of Strategic Studies affiliated to the elite Chinese National Defence University said, "This move of Russia's [suspension of CFE] indicated firstly its reluctance to make any additional unilateral compromises on the major issue of national security . . . and, secondly, its unwillingness to sit idle and remain indifferent as the US is attempting to deploy an anti-missile system in Eastern Europe in a bid to seriously affect the Russia-US strategic balance."[1] Wang noted that Russia's security concerns are bound to multiply in the prevailing scenario of "disequilibrium," where the US is "bent on seizing or using Europe to beef up its strategic superiority over Russia." Again, the Chinese Foreign Ministry spokesman on July 19 "took note of Russia's statement [on CFE] and its security concern." The spokesman went on to say that the US deployment of its ABM system will "undermine the current international strategic balance and stability. It is not conducive to regional security and mutual trust between countries."

Meanwhile, Chinese commentators have estimated that "Russia lately seems to be toughening up its diplomatic posture" and is "hardening its attitude" towards the West. The bottom line in the various Chinese assessments through the recent months is that Moscow's "hard-nosed stance" aims at putting Russia on an equal footing with the Western powers. The *People's Daily* carried an extremely significant commentary in July attributed to the Chinese Academy of Military Sciences. The commentary entitled "Strategic nuclear escalation and the multipolar world" contained some startlingly fresh thinking on the co-relation between the global strategic balance (a vestige of the Soviet-American nuclear parity) and a "multipolar" world order in the 21st century. The commentary asserted: "Strategic nuclear weapons are important for the maintenance of global strategic balance and stability." It put the Russian moves in the recent months against the backdrop of a consistent approach by the US administration under George W. Bush in the direction of seeking absolute nuclear superiority. The US initiatives in testing and deploying the Anti-Ballistic Missile or ABM systems (missile defence systems) and their deployment in Central Europe were viewed as part of the overall strategy. The commentary estimated that if the US moves were not countered, it would be a matter of time before "the US could offset Russia's strategic nuclear deterrence."

Then came the punch line. The commentary underlined, "Strategic nuclear balance is very important. Today, only strategic nuclear weapons can produce a deadly threat to the United States. Therefore, in order to establish its absolute military advantage in a unipolar world, the United States has to break the strategic nuclear balance and seek absolute strategic nuclear superiority. Meanwhile, *other countries also understand that once they lose their ability to deter a nuclear attack, they will become prey for the strong and be controlled by others*. Balance helps maintain stability. Without strategic balance, the order of the multipolar world would be difficult to maintain. To this extent, the issue of strategic balance does not simply indicate a military struggle. It is actually a question of the type of world order that should be established, and a contest between unipolar and multipolar world order."[2]

As regards the geopolitics of Central Asia (and Afghanistan), therefore, China has shared concerns with Russia, especially on two aspects. First, China also harbours, like Russia does, misgivings about NATO's designs toward Central Asia. China remains appreciative of the Russian efforts to keep NATO out of Central Asia. To quote a *People's Daily* commentary recently, "Knowing by heart the strategic importance of Central Asia, NATO has spared no efforts in recent years to push forward relations with the countries in this region. But it is by no means an easy job for NATO to gain a footing, given the overwhelming traditional influence of Russia in this region, which the US and Europe can never hope to equal. By focusing on hammering out the CSTO, Russia has displayed a strong sense of opposition against NATO. Now, the low relations between Russia and NATO have added difficulty to the latter's implementation of its Central Asia strategy."[3] That is to say, at a minimum, China's interests do not collide with the Russian approach in bolstering the CSTO's reach in Central Asia. On the other hand, a CSTO-

SCO nexus would reinforce the Russian efforts in "containing" NATO to the southwestern fringes of Eurasia. Thus, Chinese interests are well served by the Russian efforts *vis-à-vis* an invigorated CSTO.

Second, it is becoming increasingly evident that both Russia and China have been thinking hard on the concept of Central Asia. The point is, it is unrealistic for Russia and China (and for the SCO) to deal with the processes which are going on in the Central Asian region without taking into consideration the developments in Afghanistan, Iran and Pakistan. As a Russian commentator recently wrote in *Nezavisimaya Gazeta*, Central Asia's southern neighbours (Afghanistan, Iran and Pakistan) hold "much greater significance for Tajikistan than the squabbling within Kazakhstan's elite."

Arguably, SCO is feeling the compulsion already to visualise that Central Asia as a distinct community has more to do with history – its ancient, medieval and Soviet history – than with the pressing contemporary realities. The SCO has to come to terms with the reality that even though Central Asia and South Asia used to belong to different geopolitical templates until quite recently, this is no longer so, especially after 9/11 provided the opportunity to establish a long term presence in Afghanistan and to gain a significant leap in its relations with the Central Asian states.

After consolidating its presence in Afghanistan, US policy toward Central Asia has shifted gear. Through different, flexible modes of cooperation in the fields of security, transportation and energy as well as through the continued efforts to bring about "regime change" in the region, the US hopes to remodel the region. Meanwhile, the continuous expansion of the US influence in South Asia has come handy in this effort, as Afghanistan is a vital link that can connect Central Asia with South Asia. Washington has of late taken greater interest in the South Asian regional cooperation by seeking observer status in SAARC.

IRAN SEEKS OUT SCO

All the same, the SCO is increasingly bound to feel the need to evolve its own "Great Central Asia" strategy, which also includes Iran and Afghanistan, and to some extent even Pakistan. This may already be happening, and it may have got in fact reflected in two or three directions at the recent SCO summit in Bishkek. First, Iran is making a determined bid to secure full membership of the SCO. Tehran submitted its formal application to the host country Kyrgyzstan in April. In the usual course, such a formal move would have taken place on the basis of prior consultations with the SCO member states. Conceivably, a consensus is slowly developing within the SCO, if it hasn't already developed, on the issue of Iran's membership. Significantly, Iranian President Mahmoud Ahmedinejad attended the SCO summit meeting in Bishkek. Admittedly, Russian-Iranian relations are presently going through a rough patch over the delay in the completion of the Bushehr nuclear power plant. Indeed, Russia has "politicized" the issue and is unlikely to despatch the nuclear fuel for Bushehr so long as the Iran nuclear file is lying open, even though an estimated 95 per cent of the nuclear power plant's construction is complete. Despite the chill in Russian-American relations, Washington and Moscow have always closed ranks on issues affecting the preservation of the "nuclear club."

Besides, Russia has a great deal to gain by exploiting the "123" agreement on civil nuclear cooperation with the US, signed on the sidelines of the "lobster summit" on July 2, which is a major concession by Washington, allowing Russia to set up facilities for reprocessing spent nuclear fuel of US origin on commercial terms – a highly lucrative business indeed. In immediate terms, Washington's concession has opened the way for Russia to reprocess the spent fuel of US origin from South Korea and Taiwan. But, at the same time, the fracas over Bushehr is in a curious way giving Russia the handle to stall any further move by the US in the United Nations Security Council to push a new sanctions resolution against Iran. Moscow-based commentators have highlighted the current visit by the IAEA inspectors to the Arak heavy water plant as a "real breakthrough" and as evidence that "Iranians are ready to give the IAEA exhaustive answers." Despite the persisting differences over Bushehr, Moscow has taken a stance that is favourable to Tehran on the Iran nuclear issue. This became apparent as recently as September when the Kremlin signalled that it wouldn't back any US move in the UN Security Council imposing tougher sanctions on Iran. A senior Kremlin official has been quoted as saying, "As far as Iran's nuclear programme is concerned, we have passed resolutions in the UN. So far, it's enough. There are certain movements on the part of Iran, certainly as regards the IAEA. We cooperate with the US on Iran patiently, [although] it may not be as actively as [the US] would like."[4]

The conclusion we should draw is that, evidently, Bushehr is not the sum total of Russia-Iran relations. Both countries are pragmatic enough to realise that. Indeed, both countries are under compulsion to control any damage to their bilateral cooperation. Russia has shared interests with Iran in the Caspian and Central Asia. Iran is the only Caspian power, arguably, with which Russia has total identity of views as regards the inadmissibility of involvement by extra-regional powers (read US and NATO) in issues of the security of the Caspian region. Russia has to work closely with Iran at the summit of the Caspian littoral states scheduled to take place in Tehran in mid-October 2007. President Vladimir Putin is scheduled to pay his first visit to Iran on October 16.

General Bordyuzha might have spoken with a swagger when he recently invited Iran to join the CSTO as a member country. But the proposition wasn't entirely lacking in seriousness, either. During the visit of the Kyrgyz Foreign Minister Kadyrbek Sarbayev to Tehran on July 15, the influential chairman of the Security and Foreign Policy Committee of the Iranian Majlis, Ala'eddin Broujerdi strongly criticized the intrusive regional policies of the US in Central Asia. He roundly condemned the US for plotting to destabilize the Central Asian region. Interestingly, Broujerdi called for the exclusion of extra-regional security organizations from Central Asia. Broujerdi's stance as regards Central Asian security was almost dittos that of Russia and China.[5]

SCO: PROBLEMS AND PROSPECTS

In sum, there is a congruence of interests between Russia and Iran in cooperating within the SCO framework. But what are SCO's future prospects as a security organization?

If optimism is a force multiplier, as former US Secretary of State Colin Powell once said, it worked well so far for SCO. There were times in the past 7 years when it seemed doubtful if the SCO would pull through, beating back the all-out American assault on its credibility. It is certainly a measure of the SCO's success that the United States and Japan are knocking at its door for gaining "observer" status. But for Beijing and Moscow, the two capitals that jealously guarded the SCO and nursed it through its infancy, optimism wasn't the entire story behind the organization's success. Everything depended on their mutual relations, too. Fortuitously, Sino-Russian relations, which have had a difficult history during the past half-century in particular, have recently touched an almost unparalleled level of mutual understanding. That indeed helped SCO gain flesh and blood. In the past half a century, Sino-Russian relations haven't been as fraternal as they are today. To quote from an editorial by *Financial Times*, "On the face of it, SCO is everything that Richard Nixon and Henry Kissinger – who sought to keep Russia and China apart – tried to prevent."[6]

In an overarching way, however, the massive shift in the templates of great power politics in the recent years also has provided impetus for the SCO's growing clout. Matters are moving in such a direction today that, arguably, if the SCO didn't exist, Russia and China would have reason to discover one. Nothing brings this home better than the deliberation with which Russian President Vladimir Putin chose the press conference at the fag end of the SCO's first-ever military manoeuvres, "Peace Mission 2007," to make the dramatic one-line announcement, "I have decided that Russia's strategic aviation will resume patrols on a permanent basis." Putin said with his uncanny sense of timing, "At midnight today, August 17, 14 strategic missile carriers, support and refuelling aircraft took off from seven air force bases in different parts of the Russian Federation and began a patrol involving a total of 20 aircraft. As from today, such patrols will be carried out on a regular basis. These patrols are strategic in nature."[7]

SHADOW OF NEW COLD WAR

Russia has, in essence, resumed a practice that it had unilaterally suspended in 1992 with the collapse of the Soviet Union. It just happened to be on the day the SCO's first-ever military manoeuvres concluded! Conceivably, the "new cold war" appeared, like Banquo's ghost in Shakespeare's *Macbeth*, as the unsolicited guest at the SCO's summit meeting in the Kyrgyz capital Bishkek on August 16-17.

Where does the SCO fit in the "new cold war"? The question can take different forms. A variant would be, "Is SCO turning into a NATO-like military alliance?" The core issue is the extent to which Russia and China would have common concerns and shared interests in the period ahead as the chill continues to deepen in Russia's relations with the West.

Curiously, it is from the Chinese side that we get a detailed version of the two rounds of talks between Chinese President Hu Jintao and President Putin on the sidelines of the SCO summit. Briefing the Chinese journalists accompanying Hu, Foreign Minister Yang Jiechi gave an upbeat account of the strategic ties that exist between China and Russia. According to *People's Daily*, Yang identified "mapping out Sino-Russian ties and upgrading bilateral strategic coordination" as one concrete outcome of Hu's "major diplomatic manoeuvring in the Eurasian region." Yang said Chinese and Russian leaders held "in-depth and candid discussions about strategic security cooperation as well as major international and regional issues. . . . They agreed to lose no time in working out the mid- and long-term plans for Sino-Russian regional cooperation. . . .

[They] agreed to further implement the Sino-Russian strategic security negotiations . . . and to join forces to tackle other major security issues, in a concerted effort to safeguard the strategic interests of both countries. [They] held an in-depth exchange of views on major global and regional issues such as the development of the SCO, how to bring the United Nations into fuller play, and have reached a broad consensus. Their consensus will . . . raise the Sino-Russian strategic cooperation partnership to a still higher level."[8]

What stands to reason from the above is that the two leaderships may have in all probability for the first time discussed the common challenge facing the two countries, emanating out of the US plans to deploy the missile defence systems in Central Europe and the Asia-Pacific region. When asked about it, Russian Foreign Minister Sergey Lavrov left the topic delightfully vague. According to the Russian media, he said although Russia and China had not yet considered cooperation in missile defence, the two countries "share a vision of how to provide security." Lavrov added, "We and China are analysing the US global missile defence plans targeting Europe and the East."

Significantly, the government-owned *China Daily* featured a lengthy article on this subject four days after Hu's meeting with Putin. Authored by Fu Mengzi, Vice-President of the Chinese Institute of Contemporary International Relations, the article entitled "Signs point to rekindling of Cold War mentality" noted that apart from the proposed US deployments in Poland and the Czech Republic, "US is now working with Japan to advance the development of BMD [anti-ballistic missile] systems in the Far East." The article assessed that for the US, its global hegemony is no less important than its ongoing "war on terror," and this is because "the rise of non-Western powers is becoming a main trend in global politics and Russia happens to be one of those powers with a superpower's capability to rival the US in its strategic nuclear stockpile. Even though it is not the Soviet Union, Russia is still a strategic nuclear superpower next to the US. It surely will not sit idle while the US tightens the noose around its neck." The article estimates that the US is getting paranoid that the "real threat" to it comes not from terrorism but from "major power challenges." Fu concludes, "That is why NATO is still hell-bent on growing larger . . . and the US is working hard on energising the old military alliance in addition to building an 'alliance of the willing', with an obsession in forging military relations with non-allies." In sum, then, "We are watching the rekindling of the Cold War mentality in Washington's efforts to find allies and partners while beefing up its military presence in the Asia-Pacific region, East Europe and South Asia, apart from occupying Iraq indefinitely."[9]

"NATO OF THE EAST"

The SCO summit in Bishkek adopted a declaration on international security and stability, which contained thinly veiled criticism of the US global strategy. The declaration repudiated "unilateralism" and "double standards;" it emphasized "multilateralism," "strict observance of international law," and the lead role of the United Nations. Significantly, it said SCO "always stood for strengthening strategic stability." Equally, the declaration underlined that the SCO would resolutely counter the NATO and the West poaching on the Central Asian pond. It said, "The security and stability of Central Asia mainly depends on the strength of the states within the region, which may further be guaranteed on the basis of the existing regional organizations."

The Bishkek summit heard further denials that the SCO would develop into a political-military organization. Putin said, "As for the military component, it is not a military component as such but rather a counter-terrorism component. . . . I repeat that the military component is not the dominant and most important part of the SCO. Moreover, the SCO is not a closed organization. It is not a bloc organization. We hold military training exercises not only with the SCO member states but also with other countries, including with NATO member countries." Clearly, if SCO is developing into a "NATO of the east," that can only happen in the fullness of time, quite a long while from now. But, in the meanwhile, security cooperation within the SCO has intensified and is assuming new dimensions. To be sure, the possibility of the organization evolving into a full-fledged security grouping in the future cannot be ruled out.

In the short term, we may even expect an expanded framework of military cooperation, which would include different formats for forward basing and equipment propositioning. The turning point to be watched would be if and when the SCO assumes mutual security obligations among its members. On a common security policy, SCO's summit in 2006 had agreed that in the event of a threat to regional peace, stability and security, SCO member countries would enter into consultations immediately for making an effective response to the emergency. But the decision stopped short of a military assistance article as such, similar to what is spelt out in the NATO Charter. Having said that, without doubt, Peace Mission 2007 took on the trappings of a military drill rather than a counter-terrorist operation. The drill testified to the military coordination and synchronization going on within the SCO in the recent past. The fact that the exercises coincided with the political summit, and the extraordinary joint presence of the SCO leaders at the concluding stage of the manoeuvrings altogether conveyed a big political message. More importantly, SCO deliberately intended to convey such a message. Putin proposed at the Bishkek gathering that the SCO military exercises could be made into a regular feature of the organization's activities.

Again, the Bishkek summit marks one more step toward the SCO's evolution into a "supra-regional" organization. It has gained observer status at the UN; it is forging links with sister organizations like ASEAN. That is to say, SCO is incrementally placing itself on the same political pedestal as, say, the OSCE, and has a military profile somewhat resembling NATO's.

Indications are that China has finally concurred with the Russian proposal for establishing a partnership between the Collective Security Treaty Organization and the SCO. In this context, Secretary General of the CSTO, General Nikolai

Bordyuzha, is on record that the two organizations are well on the way to signing a protocol formalizing their cooperation and, furthermore, that they might in future hold joint military training. The SCO joint communiqué issued in Bishkek says, "The heads of states expressed support for expanding contacts between the SCO and the CSTO with the aim of coordinating efforts to reinforce regional and international security, and to counter new challenges and threats." Of course, there is a lot of overlap in the membership of the two organizations. Five of the seven CSTO member states are in the SCO, while five of the six SCO member states are in the CSTO. Similarly, there are overlaps in the spheres of responsibility of the two organizations. What may well happen in the short run is that a kind of division of labour may be decided upon. The SCO may focus on the range of so-called "new threats" rather than on the conventional form of military threats, while the CSTO (which is, incidentally, developing a rapid reaction force similar to NATO's), would maintain a common air defence system, training of military personnel, arms procurement, etc.

US MEETS SCO CHALLENGE

Russia's interest in stepping up the security cooperation within the SCO is undoubtedly increasing. Tajikistan President Imomali Rakhmon made an intriguing suggestion in his speech at the Bishkek summit that since the CSTO and SCO duplicate each other on several issues, they could be merged into a single organization.

How does the West tackle the SCO's "challenge"? Arguably, the West doesn't necessarily have to see the SCO as an antagonist. The stability and security of Central Asia, which is the core mission of the SCO, is as much in the West's interests as Russia's or China's. The modern-day "foreign devils on the Silk Road" – drug traffickers, Islamic warriors or plain terrorists – are as much of concern to the West's security as to the SCO member countries'. On the face of it, there is much merit in what the *Financial Times* counselled: "The SCO should be a stepping stone to Central Asia's engagement with the rest of the world, not just a jointly owned subsidiary of Moscow and Beijing."

But we live in the real world. In the same week that the SCO leaders met in Bishkek, Moscow publicized the deployment of its most modern S-400 air defence system around Moscow. And, two Bear-H strategic bombers set off from Russia on a patrol mission over flying Guam in the Pacific, home to a US strategic bomber base.

The US efforts to weaken the SCO will continue. The efforts may even be stepped up. By current indications, Washington is moving on the basis of the assessment that the SCO is still some way from becoming a strategic alliance and there is still time to weaken it before an opposition bloc actually takes shape.

The US is focusing on Russia, while there is no immediate fear of a rising China. Whereas the strategic "threat" that Russia poses is a current one, the potential threat from China will be a matter at least 15-20 years away. Besides, the US estimates that it has sufficient leverage *vis-à-vis* China. On the other hand, Russian-American relations have touched a new low, especially as Russia's recovery is accelerating and correspondingly, Russia's strategic might is reviving. Moscow has announced that it is embarking on an ambitious upgradation plan in its strategic nuclear capabilities that is designed to negate the effectiveness of the US's ABM systems. The plan features Tu-160 strategic bombers of the air force; the strategic missile force's land-based Topol-M ICBMs (inter-continental ballistic missiles); and Project 941 (Typhoon) strategic nuclear submarines of the Navy. Meanwhile, Russia is developing its own fifth-generation missile defence system, while at the same time expanding its missile defence network in its "near abroad" in Belarus, Armenia and Kazakhstan. Also, Moscow is speeding up the development of new ICBMs and realigning its strategic warheads. On July 14, the Kremlin announced that it was suspending the implementation of the Conventional Armed Forces in Europe Treaty. Simply put, Russia is determined to keep up its Soviet era strategic parity with the US.

By the end of 2006, the Russian economy had recovered to

its 1991 level before the collapse of the Soviet Union. Surplus resources are once again available to keep the military machine running. As Fu wrote in *China Daily*, "Its [Russia's] economy has been undeniably recovering after it hit rock bottom as a result of the 'shock therapy' following the end of the Cold War. The country has been profiting from high oil prices on the world market in recent years. The influx of oil and gas dollars has pumped up the country's confidence." Russia's post-Soviet transformation hasn't followed the script that Washington had written for it. Again, to quote Fu, "Moscow no longer feels it has to behave in deference to the US. . . . Russians are now ready to say whatever they want, like what Putin did at the European security summit in Munich." Thanks to Putin's massive popularity – rating above 80 per cent – Washington's hue and cry about "authoritarianism" isn't frightening the Kremlin. Russia is bent on rebuilding its traditional empirical power.[10]

Therefore, the fundamental objective of the US regional strategy in Central Asia is to weaken Russian influence in a region, which constitutes Russia's "soft underbelly," no matter Russia's legitimate interests there. The strategy works on different planes *vis-à-vis* different protagonists. Thus, Washington follows a differentiated approach toward China, aimed at creating tensions within SCO. Washington has been probing a limited arrangement with Beijing on the basis of their perceived "common interest" as energy consuming countries interested in opening Central Asian energy to alternative export routes outside Moscow's influence. Secondly, the US diplomacy projects Russian objective within SCO as aiming at tying China down within a formal alliance structure. Admittedly, Russian interest in increased security cooperation within SCO easily lends itself to such American projection. On the whole, the American strategy is predicated on the assumption that there are fundamental contradictions in Russo-Chinese relations that can be exploited.

US WOOING INDIA

On the other hand, in New Delhi, for instance, which Washington increasingly sees as its junior partner in the pursuit of its Central Asia policy, US diplomacy harps on China's growing influence in Central Asia and the thickening strategic cooperation between Russia and China. This projection principally aims at playing on India's latent sense of rivalry with China.

The Indian strategic community, which is already worked up to a frenzy by gnawing anxieties over China's phenomenal rise, is only too willing to lap up the US doomsday scenario, and to work with the US in countering China's regional influence anywhere in Asia. The mood in Delhi works splendidly well for the US interests insofar as a watchful India which resents the thickening strategic ties between Russia and China also makes it a point to incrementally distance itself from Russia. Of course, the collateral damage to the traditional bonds of friendship and cooperation between India and Russia meets the core objective of US diplomacy.

Ironically, not too long ago, Russia used to regard India as a reliable partner in Central Asia. Russian diplomacy constantly urged India to play a proactive role in Central Asia's difficult post-Soviet transition. Russian diplomats even showed frustration that Delhi was not active in Central Asia as it could be, and ought to be. Moscow's comfort level with Delhi was such that in the Soviet era, India was one of only four fraternal countries that was permitted to maintain a consulate in the Central Asian region. However, despite the pro-American tilt in India's foreign policy in the recent years, it is doubtful if Delhi sincerely believes in the viability of the US's "Great Central Asia" strategy. Delhi would know that thanks to a variety of factors, especially due to the US defeat in Iraq and Afghanistan, American stock is very low in the Central Asian steppes. The US diplomacy doesn't have any credibility with the Central Asian ruling elites.

However, the US strategy cannot work in the long run. India doesn't represent the entire South Asia. The South Asian region as a whole still lacks a basic sense of identity and experience in regional cooperation, let alone act as a model for the Central Asian states. India and Pakistan are still some distance away from dispelling the mutual mistrust in their relationship. Cross-border infrastructure projects can proceed only if harmony prevails in the intra-regional relations among the countries of South Asia. Also, Afghanistan, which is a critically important pawn in the US strategy, remains unstable.

Delhi's real mind remains inscrutable; it hardly articulates on developments concerning Central Asia; its political exchanges with Central Asia have become few and far between. Conceivably, India is keeping its counsel to itself. But, by the same token, the US can draw satisfaction that it has succeeded to a great extent in cooling India's initial fervour towards the SCO. It would seem that Washington has met with some degree of success already in persuading India to cool down its earlier passion towards the SCO. India was the only country, which was not represented at the level of head of government/state at the SCO's gala 5th anniversary summit meet in Shanghai. India has also begun dragging its feet over the Russia-China-India trilateral format. Moscow is taking note of the shift in the Indian stance.

Russia has come out openly against the US's so-called "Great Central Asia" strategy aimed at drawing the Central Asian states away from the SCO toward a regional cooperation arrangement with the South Asian region. The Russian First Deputy Foreign Minister Andrei Denisov said in an interview with the *Vremya Novostey* newspaper recently that Moscow would vehemently oppose the US strategy. "There should be no secret attempts aimed at 'pushing' some countries out of the existing system of regional relations." He added meaningfully, "Nobody opposes the strengthening of ties between states from different sub-regions in Asia, but if it is done in order to 'detach' Central Asian countries under the pretext that a geopolitical re-orientation of these countries toward the south is allegedly a 'good thing,' we will not agree with that."

Denisov's statement contains a rare rebuke of India, even if in muted implicit terms.

China has also taken note of the US strategy of courting India and pitting it against Russia and China in Central Asia so as to weaken the SCO. In June last year, *People's Daily* featured an unusually lengthy article titled "US scheming for 'Great Central Asia' strategy." The unsigned article attracted the attention of the US State Department, and prompted senior Central Asia hands in the US administration to try to counter the Chinese argument. The article argued that the US strategy has emanated out of the huge diplomatic and strategic opening that Washington has secured in the south Asian region in the most recent period. "Afghanistan is an important channel connecting Central Asia with South Asia. The anti-terrorism war has won for the US full right to speak on the situation in Afghanistan. . . . In recent years, the US has attached great importance to its South Asia operation and has been vigorously supporting India as its strategic ally in South Asia. . . . The 'Great Central Asia' strategy put forward by the US has provided both India and Pakistan with an opportunity to participate in the affairs of Central Asia." The article estimated that the US strategy is to "change the external strategic focus of Central Asia from the current Russia-and-China oriented partnership to cooperative relations with the South Asian countries . . . [to] break the long-term Russian dominance in the Central Asian area, [to] split and disintegrate the cohesion of the SCO and gradually establish US dominance in the new plate of Central and South Asia." The article implicitly warned that the US strategy would face resistance. "Afghanistan is the most critical pawn in the 'Great Central Asia' strategy. Currently, the US and Afghan central governments have very limited control over the situation in Afghanistan. Taliban remnants are still remaining. . . . According to the 'Great Central Asia' strategy, most major transport infrastructure and pipelines will pass through Afghanistan. The risks are too high." The article concluded with a friendly word of caution to India that if it consorted with the US strategy, that might put strains on India's traditional friendly relations with Russia. It said, "An important part of the 'Great Central Asia' strategy is to export the energy from Central Asia to South Asia. However, the total energy reserves and current exploiting capacity in the Central Asian region is quite limited. A large part of it is under the control of Russia. To export energy to the South Asian countries will inevitably cause conflicts with Russia."[11]

SCO EYES HINDU KUSH

The rationale of the SCO having to move south from the Central Asian region is thus obvious if the US strategy is to be effectively countered. Parallel to the SCO's strategy involving Iran, therefore, the summit in Bishkek has come up with new initiatives towards Afghanistan as well. Again, both Russia and China view with growing concern the deepening crisis in Afghanistan.

To quote from a *People's Daily* commentary in early June, "The 'Taliban phenomenon' has produced grave concern . . . its resurgence has severely challenged the authority of the Afghan government. . . . Taliban has grown more robust . . . taking full advantage of local feelings of dissatisfaction over living conditions and anti-US sentiments. . . . Taliban has galvanized its link-up with al-Qaeda remnants. . . . Afghanistan is at the risk of becoming the second Iraq."[12]

Russian thinking has also been virtually on a similar track, too. In fact, Moscow has gone a step further and openly questioned the continued rationale of the US's monopoly over conflict resolution in Afghanistan. The major review of the Russian foreign policy, undertaken by the Foreign Ministry in Moscow on the directions of President Putin in the early part of this year underlined Russia's resentment that under the fig leaf of relevant UN resolutions, Washington was in the driving seat in Afghanistan, navigating whichever way it fancied in terms of American geopolitical interests. The survey's recommendations pointed out that there existed an "objective basis for arriving at an agreed option of demonopolization of the political settlement in the country, and for the enlistment of all of Afghanistan's neighbours without exception in it."[13] The reference was no doubt to the exclusive condominium operating in Afghanistan, involving Washington, London and Islamabad.

Moscow, like Beijing, is keen to adopt a two-track approach. First, it will endeavour to work closely on a bilateral track with the government headed by Hamid Karzai. The visit by Foreign Minister Sergey Lavrov to Kabul signified an intensification of Russian diplomacy towards the Afghan problem. At the same time, Moscow is also looking for a multilateral approach involving the CSTO. Both Russia and China are greatly worried about the Taliban's resurgence in Afghanistan, though Russian statements have been more forthright. Russian Deputy Foreign Minister Alexander Grushko said in an interview with a Russian newspaper, "It is not in our interests that the Taliban re-establish control of the country, the more so since that would threaten other countries with instability."[14]

Russian commentators have frontally attacked the idea of the US differentiating "moderate Taliban." A leading Russian military analyst, Nikolai Khorunzhy wrote in July, "Aware that the military face-off cannot be solved by force alone, Afghanistan's leadership is trying, at NATO's suggestion, to open a dialogue with the Taliban in the hopes of winning its least repulsive leaders over to its side. The alliance is forgetting the counter-terrorist aims it proclaimed at the outset of the military intervention and is ready to make a deal with those whom only yesterday it described as sponsors of terrorists. This belies its claim that it plays a special, global role in the struggle against today's threats."[15]

Significantly, CSTO Secretary General Bordyuzha suggested in July, "We [CSTO and SCO] together, including China, which makes part of the SCO, should assist in preventing the Taliban from coming to power, otherwise we will get serious problems in Afghanistan, problems for many years." Bordyzha hinted at the likelihood of an extensive involvement by the SCO in Afghanistan. He said, "Work should be conducted in all spheres, political and economic, and in rendering assistance in the formation of armed forces and law enforcement organs of the government, as well as in the fight against illegal drug trafficking."[16]

To be sure, the SCO summit meeting came up with proposals aimed at intensifying the functioning of the SCO-Afghanistan Contact Group.

The SCO has begun hitting back at the US's "Great Central Asia" strategy. It is hitting back in Afghanistan, which Washington regards as the "hub" of its strategy to link up Central Asia with South Asia. The SCO put the US on notice that it is quite capable of contesting the Anglo-American monopoly of conflict resolution in Afghanistan. The Bishkek declaration said, "The member countries are willing to participate in the efforts to normalize Afghanistan's political situation . . . as well as improve the work of the SCO-Afghanistan Contact Group." The joint communiqué issued after the Bishkek summit went a step further saying, "The (SCO) leaders also discussed the possibility of the SCO taking bigger part in the Afghanistan affairs, to contribute more to regional security and stability."

Warning bells must be ringing in Washington and London.

Putin in his speech at the SCO summit all but implied that the US and NATO have dismally failed to prevent Afghanistan from becoming an open wound infecting Central Asia. He called for reinforcing "anti-drug security belts" around Afghanistan supervised by SCO monitors. The summit decided to organize an international conference on Afghanistan next year.

The US counter-strategy towards any SCO role in Afghanistan will be by way of binding Pakistan even closer to the NATO. Pakistan's "loyalty" becomes crucial because most of the supplies for the NATO forces go through Pakistani territory. But, in turn, this makes the US's Afghan strategy even more heavily dependent on Pakistan's cooperation. One offshoot is that Washington shudders at the thought of any "regime change" to take place in Islamabad, no matter Musharraf's standing in Pakistan.

On the other hand, Washington is under compulsion to accommodate Pakistan's legitimate interests in Afghanistan. The recent "peace jirga" in Kabul in the second week of August 2007 is a step toward reaching some sort of political accommodation with the Taliban as well as for strengthening the Durand Line. According to latest reports, the US officials have already begun holding face-to-face secret meetings with the Taliban representatives in secret locations inside Pakistan. Of course, any such talks would have to be under the watchful eyes of the Pakistani intelligence.

Meanwhile, the sense of urgency is palpable in Washington to somehow seek a political settlement of the war in Afghanistan. Battle fatigue is setting in among the coalition forces in Afghanistan. It has been crystal clear that the NATO operations are going nowhere. There is growing frustration that peace is nowhere on the horizon. The 50,000-strong NATO contingent is failing in its mission to rout the Taliban and al-Qaeda. Among the coalition forces, there is growing difference of opinion over tactics and deployment. The new British government has reportedly told the US administration that in Afghanistan, the coalition forces are "winning the battles but losing the war." Among the Afghans, too, there is a growing sense of despondency about the NATO's war strategy. Last week, in an interview with the AFP news agency, former foreign minister Dr. Abdullah Abdullah said that the gap between the government and the people is widening. Growing insecurity, government inefficiency and incompetence and the absence of any development has combined to generate a mood of popular disillusion. "Today, from what I hear from the people, it is something like they are losing hope," Abdullah said.[17]

Thus, all things taken into account, Washington is gearing up for the endgame – politically engaging the Taliban. Quite obviously, the processes set in motion at the Afghan jirga in August in the direction of accommodating the Taliban in political terms are now being speeded up. It was clear from the outset that the jirga took place with the full blessings of the US government.

CERTAINTY OF CHANCE

A Taliban spokesman has been quoted as saying, "For the sake of national interests . . . we are fully ready for talks with the government. Whenever the government formally asks for negotiations, we are ready." He offered that Taliban would be willing for high-level representation at the talks with the government. He has spoken of minimal "pre-conditions," which would, presumably, relate to an assurance from the Americans that the Taliban who show up from their hideouts for reconciliation wouldn't be arrested and despatched to Guantanamo Bay.[18]

Thus, as the surrealist would say, the certainty of chance is that an "intra-Afghan dialogue" is finally getting under way. A sure sign is that the United Nations has also got into the act. The UN Secretary General's Special Envoy, Tom Koenigs has voiced support for talks with the Taliban. Koenigs told a German daily, "So far many have said we do not negotiate with terrorists, meaning also the Taliban. However, the Taliban movement is multi-faceted. You cannot lump all of them together." Recently, a German government spokesman, Thomas Steg had hinted at possible talks with "moderate and reasonable" Taliban elements. Koenigs has since appealed for a total cessation of violence across Afghanistan on September 21 to mark the International Day of Peace. He claimed, "The response has been vast, and it continues to grow. Help us make peace in Afghanistan real."

When asked about these trends at a Kabul press conference, the visiting US Deputy Secretary of State John Negroponte wasn't dismissive about the Taliban's offer of talks. Nor did he mention the fact that the Taliban was a "terrorist" organization under US law and Washington wouldn't negotiate with it. Instead, he said, "We would want to know the view of the government of Afghanistan. Whatever happens, these talks by the Taliban should be handled in such a way by the government of Afghanistan that it does not in any way undermine or prejudice all the important political, social and economic accomplishments that have occurred in this country."

On the face of it, an "intra-Afghan dialogue" has been an

imperative need all along. But the question today is, can this "intra-Afghan dialogue" be made to stick at a time when the situation in Pakistan itself is fast spinning out of anybody's control? Yet, the crisis in Pakistan is still unfolding and an increasingly destabilising situation is developing. And we seem to forget that Pakistan has nuclear weapons; for the first time, it seems within the realms of possibility that these nuclear weapons could fall into the hands of the Islamic militants. The focus today ought to be on an "intra-Pakistani dialogue." As the veteran Russian "orientalist," former Prime Minister Yevgeny Primakov recently wrote, "It seems to me that Washington, which is currently preoccupied with deploying its military units and missile defence elements in the newly admitted NATO member countries, could 'miss the boat' in Pakistan. . . . Is it not time for the US to start consultations with Russia, India and China regarding Pakistan?"[19]

Taliban's political rehabilitation at this juncture is certain to cause disquiet among regional powers. Iran's resistance to the Taliban would seem to be the hardest to overcome. Everything depends on the US's hostility toward Iran. If the US-Iran standoff erupts into a military confrontation, that is bound to have its reverberations in Afghanistan. The new head of Iran's Revolutionary Guards, General Muhammad Ali Jaafari said this week, "The Revolutionary Guards have identified all the weak points of the enemy in Iraq and Afghanistan and based on this have consolidated the defensive capabilities of our country. And if the enemy [US] wants to take any impudent action, Iran will for sure give a decisive and teeth-breaking response."

Russia and the Central Asian countries would be particularly concerned. They have consistently seen a connection between Islamic extremism in Central Asia and the Caucasus and the Taliban. Chechen Internet sites even today glorify the Taliban. It is an established fact that Uzbek extremists are engaged in the fighting in Afghanistan. Central Asian states in particular will view the appeasement of the Taliban with great concern. Uzbekistan President Islam Karimov, in his speech at the SCO's Bishkek summit, called for the West to "demilitarize" Afghanistan.

Russia and the Central Asian states would worry that once the radical movement is allowed entry into mainstream political life, Afghanistan could get "Talibanized." The ground reality is that the Taliban is today by far the best-organized force in Afghanistan. It can easily eclipse the other groups and establish its dominance. From Moscow's point of view, such views will surely push Russia and the Central Asian countries closer together. They will look for the CSTO (and SCO) to provide the defence line against any threat of creeping "Talibanization" across the Amu Darya. But they would be essentially getting back to the situation prevailing in the 1999-2000 period.

Russia projects its concern essentially in terms of self-defence. But the bottom line is that Russia wants to have a role in Afghanistan. There is no question that Russia wouldn't want to bring its troops into Afghanistan. But Russia would like the US (and the West) to make use of "Moscow's experience in Afghanistan" (to quote Primakov).

ENERGY WAR INTENSIFIES

From all these perspectives, the time has come for the SCO to seriously ponder over its future role in Afghanistan. But, having said that, we would do well to remember that the rivalries in gaining access to the region's vast energy resources and in securing the transportation routes for evacuating the energy to the world market is a constant theme in the geopolitics of the region.

A key agenda item at the SCO's Bishkek summit was the role of Iran in energy cooperation. This is a topic of common interest to Russia and China. On its part, Russia stands to gain if Iran's energy flows are diverted toward the Asian market rather than finding their way to the European market. Russia has been watching with unease the renewed efforts by Turkey and the European Union (despite apparent US reservations) to line up Iran both as a gas supplier and as a conduit for Turkmen gas for filling up the proposed Nabucco pipeline, which rivals Russia's energy projects in the Balkans and southern Europe. In mid-July, Turkey and Iran signed a memorandum of understanding in this respect. Last week, Turkey followed up with an agreement with Italy and Greece, which would be the consumers of the Iranian gas.

Russia would hope that Iran didn't commit to the Nabucco pipeline. Russia has an added interest in encouraging Iran to become an energy supplier for China insofar as thereby the potential for any Russian-Chinese conflict of interests over the Central Asian energy reserves (especially in Turkmenistan) diminishes. In fact, the proposed Chinese gas pipeline leading to Turkmenistan can be easily extended to Iran. Finally, of course, Iran is an important player in any grand Russian strategy involving any variant of the idea of a 'Gas OPEC'. This complicated equation explains why the US remains staunchly opposed to Iran's membership of the SCO. Washington factors that a potential SCO "energy club" (first mooted by Putin two years ago) will remain incomplete so long as Iran and Turkmenistan do not become part of it.

In both respects, Washington can derive satisfaction from the outcome of the Bishkek summit. The SCO seems unprepared for the present to grant Iran full membership. Unsurprisingly, SCO doesn't want to get sucked into the Iran-US standoff with its potential ramifications for Russian-American and Sino-American relations if a military confrontation takes place, which cannot be ruled out. On the contrary, SCO is overtly keen to grant membership to Turkmenistan but President Gurbanguly Berdymukhammedov is playing "hard-to-get."

Just ahead of the SCO summit, US Assistant Secretary of State for Economic, Energy and Business Affairs Daniel Sullivan arrived in Ashgabat urging Berdymukhammedov to diversify Turkmenistan's energy export routes and promising deeper cooperation with American companies. "We believe that increased diversification of energy routes, buyers and suppliers are in Turkmenistan's long-term energy security interest. . . . Nations should never be left with only one option, one market, one trading partner, and one vital infrastructure link. . . . We are encouraging American companies to invest in Turkmenistan to help your country grow," Sullivan exhorted.

At any rate, contrary to earlier indications, the Bishkek summit put off Turkmenistan's admission even though Berdymukhammedov attended as a special invitee. The day after the SCO summit concluded, coincidence or not, Washington announced that it was granting funds for undertaking feasibility study for a trans-Caspian gas pipeline project from Turkmenistan.

Moscow and Beijing should have reason to worry. Soon after the SCO summit meeting in Bishkek, Chinese President Hu Jintao and Kazakhstan President Nurusultan Nazarbayev agreed to build an oil pipeline from Turkmenistan's Caspian shore to China across Kazakhstan, which will be the second leg of the Atasu-Alashankou oil pipeline with a throughput capacity of 10 million metric tonnes annually and is expected to come on stream in 2009. Only 3 days prior to the Hu-Nazarbayev meeting, Kyrgyz and Tajik leaders had separately canvassed with Hu in Bishkek (on the sidelines of the SCO summit meeting) that a section of yet another planned Turkmenistan-China gas pipeline should be built on their territories.

Both Russia and China would feel uneasy that Turkmenistan is coming under American influence. Moscow would count on the forthcoming summit meeting of the Caspian littoral states to be held in Tehran on October 18 as an occasion for clarifying equations. Russia, Kazakhstan and Turkmenistan will take part in the summit. The Iranian hosts can be expected to lend a hand in dissuading the Turkmen leader from trading with the Great Satan in the overall interests of regional stability.

AMERICAN HEADACHES

The SCO summit meeting in Bishkek, nonetheless, posed challenges for the United States from various angles. The coming together of the CSTO and the SCO, once the cooperation gets formalized in the coming months, would be a double setback to the US regional policies. Both are entities that are anathema to the US geopolitical interests. The US strove to stifle these two organizations in their infancy, but is instead now seeing them gather new strength. The US game plan projecting NATO into the Central Asian region has indeed run into a formidable obstacle. The US dilemma is acute. For, unless NATO expands into Central Asia, there can be no full "encirclement" of either Russia or China. It is senseless if NATO remains stuck in Southern Caucasus.

Indeed, NATO's credibility is at stake, too. As things stand, NATO's "transformation" isn't progressing smoothly. Afghanistan has become a lump in the NATO's throat. NATO can't spit it out, nor can it swallow. It is disfiguring NATO. No amount of propaganda can hide the reality that the Afghan people are increasingly viewing NATO as an occupation force. Apart from insufficient troop strength, NATO commanders are in desperate need of intelligence.

The US's "pull" within NATO is also on the decline. The change of leadership in France, Germany and Britain doesn't seem to work quite the way Washington expected. Therefore, Washington will do its utmost to ward off the SCO's "encroachment" onto the Afghan turf. Washington will count on Karzai to smother the SCO's overtures. The US predicament will be that on the face of it, the SCO initiative on Afghanistan cannot be questioned. Karzai would also look rather foolish if he were to spurn an offer of help from the SCO. After all, the SCO has a legitimate interest in effectively stabilising the situation in Afghanistan since the stability of the Central Asian region is linked to it in many respects. On the other hand, Washington's grip over the Kabul set-up will incrementally weaken once Afghanistan develops an "SCO connection." Washington should be extremely wary, since Afghans are quite adept at playing their optimal role in the Great Game. Most important, the US will increasingly find itself under compulsion to perform as a "team player," which suits neither its geo-strategy nor its standing as the sole superpower.

In all this, Pakistan remains an unpredictable player given the fluidity of its internal situation as indeed Islamabad's keenness to work closely with the SCO and China. Most of the supplies for the NATO forces in Afghanistan pass through Pakistan. It will be quite an irony if a situation develops where the US ends up doing all the fighting in Afghanistan, while the SCO gains in public adulation among the Afghan people and in the wider region as a 'nation-builder'.

Least of all, Washington knows that SCO's involvement in the Afghan problem ultimately means Russia will be making a big re-entry into the Hindu Kush, apart from foiling the US's grand design to steer the NATO as a global security organization with global partners. Curiously, on July 17, Tajikistan announced that an agreement has been concluded providing for the deployment of Russian combat aircraft on the Ayni airbase outside Dushanbe. Indications are that in the first instance Russia will deploy four each Su-25 aircraft and Mi-24 and Mi-8 helicopters. The Russian deployment will be within the CSTO framework. Moscow just about stumped the last lingering hope of gaining a toehold in Tajikistan – for the time being, at least.

GREAT GAME ACCELERATING

It is extremely rare that the geopolitics of an entire region comes to be encapsulated within a single occasion. To be sure, the ceremony on the banks of the Pyanj River marking the opening of the first ever bridge connecting Tajikistan and Afghanistan provided a moveable feast for politicians, diplomats, media persons and strategic thinkers alike. Anyone even remotely interested in the Great Game took note. The US President George W. Bush made it a point amidst the distractions over Iraq to depute a cabinet-rank official to be present at the bridge opening ceremony on August 26 in Tajikistan.

What is there after all in a 670-metre bridge? Hitherto a sporadic ferry service connected the Tajik town of Nizhny Pyanj with the Afghan town of Shir Khan Bandar. The torrential currents in the river didn't allow the ferry to operate for months at a stretch once the glaciers melted in the Pamirs and flooded the tributaries. The new bridge can easily handle as many as 1,000 trucks per day.

Strictly speaking, US Secretary of Commerce Carlos Gutierrez didn't have to come all the way to witness the commissioning of the US$ 37 million project. But the US administration evidently regarded this as a showcase project. Mr. Gutierrez said the bridge would become "the widest connection between Afghanistan and the rest of the world." That was an interesting enough diplomatic statement – co-relating Afghanistan to its northern neighbours. But, more important, he went on to describe the bridge as a "physical and symbolic link between Central Asia and South Asia." The Afghan President Hamid Karzai, who was present, took a step further ahead and called it a link that "unites Central Asia with Southern and East Asia." China enters the podium.

The Tajik-Afghan bridge (built, incidentally, by the US Army Corps of Engineers) provides a microcosm of the highly complex calculus of the politics of Central Asia. Three things became abundantly clear. First, the Great Game in Central Asia not only shows no signs of abating, but it is actually accelerating. Second, Washington is pressing ahead with its "Great Central Asia" strategy, no matter the fluidity of the Afghan (and Pakistani) security situation. Third, Washington has knowingly facilitated for China an efficient access route leading to the markets in South Asia and the Persian Gulf. Conventional wisdom among the strategic thinkers about Sino-American rivalries in Central Asia takes a beating.

The US has not cared to hide the fact that the primary objective of the bridge on the river Pyanj was to provide Tajikistan a transportation route to the outside world bypassing Russian territory. But Tajikistan's trade with Afghanistan amounted to a paltry sum of US $ 25 million last year. Tajikistan is not a great manufacturing centre and is unlikely to be one in the near future, though rich in rare earths and minerals. It has a subsistence economy. With mountains accounting for 93 per cent of its entire territory, a potential export item would be electricity and water resources, but Tajikistan doesn't need a bridge across the Pyanj to export them.

Of late, the Great Game, which has been keenly pursued in Kazakhstan, Uzbekistan and Kyrgyzstan, has spilled over into Tajikistan and Turkmenistan. The transfer of power to a new leadership in Turkmenistan following the death of Saparmurat Niazov last December opened a window of opportunity for the US to contest the lead role established by Russia and China in accessing the country's vast resources of natural gas. That is quintessentially the brewing great power rivalry in Turkmenistan. Simply put, the US wants the new Turkmen leadership to earnestly take a second look at the 10-year old idea regarding a Trans-Caspian gas pipeline heading for the European market via Azerbaijan-Georgia-Turkey, which would cut down Europe's growing dependency on Russian energy supplies.

But what is unfolding over Tajikistan is vintage Great Game from the nineteenth century – "foreign devils on the Silk Road." Briefly, the then US Secretary of Defence Donald Rumsfeld made a tactical error of judgement in October 2001 in choosing to set up military bases in Uzbekistan and Kyrgyzstan. In a memorable visit to Dushanbe, Tajik President Rakhmon ostentatiously spread a Soviet army map in front of Rumsfeld and made an open offer that Washington could pick and choose any of the military bases that the Soviet army has built. Rumsfeld was disinterested.

But, then, hardly five years passed and the geopolitics of Central Asia had changed so dramatically that Rumsfeld, now a pensioner, must be ruing his fateful error of judgement. With the rupture in the US's relations with Uzbekistan following the uprising in Andizhan in May 2005 and the descending anarchy in Kyrgyzstan following the "Tulip revolution" (March 2001), Tajikistan's importance has increased as a gateway to Central Asia for the US influence entrenched in Afghanistan.

Tajikistan's strategic importance needs no repetition – it is a corridor leading to the turbulent Ferghana Valley; it borders Xinjiang; it is a hotbed of militant Islam; it is an oasis of Iranian

(Persian) culture; it controls the region's watersheds; it is a principal route for the drug traffickers from Afghanistan; and, it is the furthest post-Soviet military outpost for the Russian armed forces on the territory of the former USSR. Over and above, of course, Tajikistan is integral to the stabilization of Afghan politics. There are more ethnic Tajiks living in Afghanistan than in Tajikistan itself. Tajik nationalism can also be a potent weapon in the hands of Uzbekistan's adversaries. Thus, for any number of good reasons, prising away Tajikistan from the orbit of traditional Russian influence has become a key objective of the US diplomacy. Washington is pressing Japan and the European Union to take interest. The EU foreign policy chief Javier Solana visited Dushanbe in the first week of August.

The thrust of the US's so-called "Great Central Asia" strategy is to pull Tajikistan towards Afghanistan by the scruff of its neck, as it were, so that that a new dynamics will generate, which would incrementally draw the Central Asian region itself towards the South Asian countries, with Afghanistan acting as a hub or a revolving door. With the consolidation of US strategic influence in the recent years in the south Asian region, Washington estimates that its skilful midwifery in Central Asia has a fair chance of success. The US has brought in financial institutions like the World Bank and Asian Development Bank to explore the possibility of funding trans-regional projects that aim at strengthening the infrastructure and communication links between the countries of the Central Asian and South Asian region. In the US understanding, a strategic alliance between Russia and China in Central Asia within the framework of the SCO is a long way from materialising. More important, the US estimates that it can avoid a strategic alliance by balancing Russia and China individually or off each other. There is great scope available for US diplomacy to work on the differing priorities of Russia and China within the SCO.

Alexander Khramchikhin, chief analyst of Russia's Political and Military Analysis Institute, wrote in *Izvestia* newspaper recently, "Russia is clearly inclined to turn the SCO into a military-political bloc to confront and counter NATO. Moscow would like a merger of the SCO and the Collective Security Treaty Organization, but our partners are still resisting the idea. Beijing may not be entirely opposed to a military alliance, but its policy is entirely rational and pragmatic. . . . Beijing is more inclined to see the SCO's economic component as dominant. China's priority is oil and gas supplies, of course. . . . SCO is perfect for China's purposes. All SCO countries except Uzbekistan share borders with China, so energy resources can be delivered via safe land routes. . . . Another advantage of an energy market in the SCO framework is that several oil and gas suppliers (Russia, Kazakhstan and Uzbekistan, and perhaps Iran and Turkmenistan) would be competing for one buyer, China. . . . The economic format of the SCO is advantageous for China because of its powerful economy . . . From China's perspective, SCO countries are an important transit corridor for contacts [with the world market]."[20]

US-CHINA EQUATIONS

Not surprisingly, the US strategy pursues a differentiated approach toward China. The core agenda of the US policy is to create a wedge between Russia and China, which would prove the nemesis of the SCO. The point is, over the near to medium term at least, Washington doesn't perceive China's growing presence in Central Asia as presenting a pressing challenge to the US interests.

This comfort level in Washington is attributable to several factors. First, much as China has made impressive gains in Central Asia, it faces many challenges and competitors while furthering its political, diplomatic and economic presence in the region. Even assuming that Russian influence in the region is waning (which is not the case), the ground reality is that at the end of the day, the Central Asian elites feel far more at home in harbouring close ties with Russia than with China. Again, despite recent setbacks, the US still remains a major contender in the region.

So is Japan, which is fixated with the idea of countering Chinese influence in Central Asia.

Second, in the American perception, Chinese diplomatic strategy in Central Asia is mainly driven by China's domestic imperative of developing and sustaining stable and productive relations around the country's periphery so as to create a beneficial external environment within which Beijing can meaningfully address the enormous socio-political and development challenges within. Of course, China cannot be faulted if it strives to legitimise its image as a benign regional leader. In other words, the US has no reason to feel "threat perceptions" over the proactive Chinese diplomacy in Central Asia.

Third, Washington appreciates that China has several legitimate national security interests at stake in Central Asia. The huge territorial concessions that China made in settling its border dispute with the Central Asian states, and the key agreements of 1996 and 97 showed that China regarded that the region's goodwill needed to be cultivated and therefore making compromises was every bit worthwhile in China's medium and long term interests. China's obsession with the "three evils" manifest in the region (terrorism, separatism and religious extremism) is palpable.[21]

Again, the US would have no reason to quarrel with China on account of the latter keenly exploring opportunities of trade and economic cooperation with Central Asia. In fact, it suits the US regional strategy that China is increasingly figuring as a major business competitor for Russia both in the energy and non-energy sectors. For instance, there is a good possibility that China is likely to replace Russia's UC Rusal in the US$ 1.3 billion aluminium-cum-hydroelectric power project in Tajikistan.

A degree of rivalry already exists between China and Russia in gaining access to Turkmenistan's gas reserves. The fact is, as China moves up the economic ladder, it is better placed than Russia in providing much-needed capital, technology, expertise and the range of consumer goods that the Central Asian countries need. Furthermore, it is possible for the US to harmonise its Central Asia strategy with China's focus on building transportation infrastructure, especially a multilateral highway transportation infrastructure, which would only weaken Russia's Soviet era stranglehold on the region's communication links.

Finally, Washington estimates that since China's relations remain at a relatively early stage in the region, it is only through a strategic partnership with Russia that Beijing can venture into any balance-of-power games. Of course, looking further ahead, Washington and Beijing could find themselves competing for influence in Central Asia as their regional priorities continue to expand beyond immediate security concerns and touch upon Great Power influence and diplomatic strategy.

In other words, in the short term at least, the US is pursuing a careful policy to engage China in the region and assuring that China's emergence is consistent with the US interests. This indeed helps Washington to focus on the immediate task in hand, namely, to roll back Russia's traditional standing in the region which is standing right in the way of the expansion of US influence in the region. Of course, Moscow remains alert about the US ploys to create a wedge between Russia and China. It must be assumed from the Chinese commentaries also that much as Beijing keeps its thoughts to itself, it is seized of the US's strategy. The annual ARF forum, which was held in Manila in late July-early August provided a useful window of opportunity to test the temperature in the trilateral US-China-Russia equations. What emerged is that Russia is quite comfortable with the impressive growth of China's influence in the Asian region. A top commentator of the Russian official news agency *RIA Novosti* assessed, "China has once again shown that it is vital for Asian security. It is also true that the economic situation in Asia would not look good without China . . . If one country gets a bigger piece, it doesn't mean that another one will have to settle for less. Russia has also found itself in a good position because China's bigger role in Asia increases Russia's influence there." Most significantly, the Russian analyst, who is a prominent observer of Asian politics, continued, "Beijing feels more confident because it is a member of the Shanghai Cooperation Organization on a par with Moscow, and the two are jointly carrying out numerous military-technical cooperation programs. Their security is closely linked."[22]

Conceivably, Moscow would also counsel Delhi that the latter doesn't have to view the Asian security in zero-sum terms. As the Russian commentator put it, "China's success hasn't left anyone empty-handed."

INDIA SHOULDN'T SLUMBER

The bridge on the Pyanj brings out these various templates of the US's regional policy response to the growing Chinese presence in Central Asia. It is extraordinary that the US is prepared to go to any extent for undercutting the SCO and isolating Russia in Central Asia. There is no gainsaying the fact that China is going to be the single biggest beneficiary of the bridge that connects Tajikistan and Afghanistan.

Curiously, China seems to have anticipated that Tajikistan will eventually prove to be as crucial as Pakistan as a transportation route. Beijing has been paying enormous attention to Tajikistan by earmarking the bulk of its US$ 900 million export loan for SCO for its projects in Tajikistan. China's assistance to Tajikistan in the past 5-year period exceeds US$ 600 million. Trade touched a level of US$ 157 million in 2005. But the first half of 2006 alone saw a quantum jump to US$ 114 million. China is generously investing in Tajikistan's light industry.

The US-funded bridge across the Pyanj River leads in the north to China's newly developed road links with Tajikistan. It provides China's Xinjiang Autonomous Region with yet another all-weather communication link with Karachi port, which Karakorum Highway cannot. By constructing the bridge, Washington has virtually signalled that China doesn't have to necessarily depend on the SCO for developing its transportation routes to the South Asian and Persian Gulf region. In fact, the US State Department handout in Washington DC regarding the

Pyanj bridge highlights the great deliberation in the US policy by pointing out, "On the Tajik side, the bridge will connect to routes leading north, west and east through roads that Japan plans to build or modernize; on the Afghan side, it will connect to Afghanistan's nearly-completed ring road and Pakistan's port of Karachi through roads constructed with ADB financing."

There is enough food for thought here for the Indian strategic analysts rooted in their belief that China's access to the warm waters of the South Asian and Persian Gulf region would be completely antithetical to the US strategic interests. The Indian strategic community is paranoid that any act of Chinese foreign policy in India's neighbourhood is directed against India. Some have gone to the extent of decrying the Chinese moves as part of an "encirclement" of India. Some others have already outstripped everyone else by deriving a US-Indian congruence of strategic interests in keeping China's "blue water Navy" out of the Indian Ocean. They gloated that the logic of the recently held 'Malabar Exercises' in Bay of Bengal in September 2007 was an unambiguous warning to Beijing that Washington and Delhi remain shoulder to shoulder in warding off China's ascendancy in the region to the west of the Malacca Straits. They cite China's cooperation with Pakistan and Myanmar as "hard" evidence of China's ill intentions. The Tajik-Afghan bridge built by the Americans must be an eye-opener for such analysts.

What Indian analysts can overlook only at great peril to their intellectual honesty and integrity is that for China, Pakistan and Myanmar are important neighbouring countries. It is plain common sense that we cannot demand that Beijing, as a mark of friendliness toward us, should neglect to develop China's relations with its own neighbours. The fact of the matter is that unlike India, China accords the highest priority in its foreign policy to its relations with its neighbours. In certain ways, our foreign policy orientations are diametrically opposite to those of China's. Our foreign policy mandarins increasingly conduct themselves as if India belongs to the Euro-Atlantic community and that Indians, as "natural allies" of the Americans, simply happen to live in this moth-eaten part of the world.

Take, for example, China's keenness to develop the Gwadar port in Pakistan and to connect the port with a broadened Karakorum Highway, or the road network and oil pipelines and harbour development that China is undertaking in Myanmar. We cannot overlook the reality that the Gulf region accounts for almost 90 per cent of China's oil imports. China accords the highest priority for the export of its products to the booming Gulf markets and in the newly developed African markets. The routes via Pakistan or Myanmar by far shorten China's long-winded routes existing today via the Malacca Straits.

Do we really have to feel paranoid about the Chinese "designs" in this respect? Also, what prevents us from developing our own relations with the countries of our region? It is not as if China is coming in the way of India's relations with its neighbours like Myanmar or Pakistan or Nepal. As a matter of fact, there are indications that by end-2007, China may well replace the US as India's number 1 trading partner.

The Central Asian region is a glaring example of the lop-sided priorities of India's foreign policy. No serious power can ignore the regions neighbouring to it and the ring of extended regions that lie beyond it. History testifies to the importance of geography in foreign policy. Yet, India's relations with the Central Asian region are virtually in a state of neglect and disrepair. Our policy towards that critically important region can be summed up as one of "masterly inactivity."

India started off brilliantly in the early 1990s when the countries of Central Asia appeared as independent sovereign entities. Thanks to the Soviet propaganda, which unfailingly preached the idealism of Indo-Soviet friendship, India was a role model for the Central Asian states. Post-Soviet Russia, which was struggling to recover from the "shock therapy" that Boris Yeltsin inflicted, constantly pleaded with India at the political and diplomatic level to step into the vacuum in Central Asia and to play a leadership role. But India wouldn't. India's own priorities lay elsewhere. Its big power dreams didn't include a corner for the Central Asian region. India was niggardly in making investments in the region, India neglected its trade with the region, and India did nothing to develop its communication links with the region. It may sound incredible but the fact is that even today, not a single Indian airline, government or private, operates in and out of any Central Asian capital. (The furthest point from Delhi would be Almaty, which is roughly a 2-hour flight, comparable to the distance from Delhi to Hyderabad.)

But, of late, India is showing signs of falling into the US trap by gradually working itself into a frenzy over the growing Chinese influence in the Central Asian region. The SCO's annual summit meetings are becoming a veritable foreign policy challenge for India.

Should India be enthusiastic about the SCO? If it is, wouldn't that be running contrary to the US regional policy toward SCO? How far should India remain indifferent towards an organization that is so obviously impacting directly on India's interests? What would be the fate of India's relations with Russia if India disengages from the SCO? What does India do to counter Russian-Chinese cooperation that SCO represents, as it gains greater traction? These are the gnawing doubts in the foreign policy establishment in Delhi.

The 2005 SCO summit meeting brought the Indian dilemma to a boil. The SCO was celebrating its fifth anniversary in Shanghai city. The Chinese leadership took legitimate pride that the single most important regional initiative by Beijing in its post-Cold War foreign policy was turning out to be a success story. Prime Minister Manmohan Singh's presence at the summit meeting would have been a thoughtful expression of India responding to the Chinese goodwill, apart from according due recognition of the SCO's huge significance for India's foreign policy interests for decades to come.

But, in the event, at the summit in Shanghai in 2005, India was the only country among the SCO's member countries and observers that was not represented at the head of government or head of state level. The entire region took note at the glaring omission on India's part. Was it intended by New Delhi as a snub to the Chinese leadership? Was it attributable to the lack of understanding of geo-strategy by the Indian mandarins? Or, was it a deliberate decision taken in cool thinking by the Indian political leadership to "appease" the US? There are no easy answers.

All that we know is that the United Progressive Alliance government sent a loud message to the capitals in the entire Asian region – and all the way to Washington – that it was revisiting its earlier enthusiasm for the SCO. The US never wished the SCO well and would have loved to throttle the organization in its infancy. Washington must have been mightily pleased that the UPA government in Delhi was placing India on "their side" of the Asian divide.

These troubling questions about the orientations of Indian policy toward the SCO and the Central Asian region stand against a highly complicated regional backdrop. The point is, the international system on the whole is undergoing a period of transformation that is unprecedented in the past 100 years, and yet, as the former US Secretary of State Henry Kissinger recently wrote, we are only at the very outset of a very long period of adjustment. It is curious that Kissinger, a master-practitioner of the theory of the "balance of forces" in world politics should be treading so softly and warily.

It offers a salutary moral to those in the strategic community in the sequestered vistas of central Delhi who fancy that India is already a "balancer" in the international system, thanks to its diaspora in North America or its mushrooming call centres. How could we be a "balancer" in an international system that still remains embedded in the womb of time?

Nothing brings out more graphically the fluidity of the international system than the proximity developing between China and the countries belonging to the Non-Aligned Movement, or, for that matter, the bridge that the US Army has just built for facilitating China's access to the markets in South Asia and the Persian Gulf region. China realises that instead of pretending to be half a superpower, it is expedient to use the present interregnum to build diverse bridges that might prove useful for all seasons. China has no mental blocs regarding NAM. After all, wisdom lies in making use of what is readily available. China is right in estimating that there is a world community beyond the US, Japan or Australia. What is clear from China's example is that India is only one among many countries in the world community today that faces choices of ideology, path of development and diplomatic strategy. At a minimum, this calls for an open, inclusive approach on India's part.

Why is the SCO so important for India?

First and foremost, it is a security organization that focuses on regional security and stability. Fighting terrorism, religious extremism and political separatism forms the core of the SCO's agenda. In this sphere, India has shared concerns with the SCO member countries.

Second, SCO is comfortably large enough for a country of India's height and girth to take its due place. There is so single overbearing presence in the tent. On the contrary, the SCO is overtly keen that India should grace the tent by its presence. All decisions taken by the SCO are on the basis of consensus. The SCO is adamant that it will not preach or prescribe any particular way of life to the world community.

Third, SCO stands for a democratized world order based on multilateralism and respect of international law. It gives primacy to the United Nations in world affairs. It makes no distinction between countries big and small. It believes that security is indivisible. But it respects national sovereignty in the conduct of international relations. India should completely feel at home in the SCO's environs.

Fourth, SCO can creatively supplement India's "Look East" policy of engaging the countries of the Southeast Asian and the Asia Pacific regions. At the Bishkek summit, in fact, SCO has further strengthened its linkages with the ASEAN.

Fifth, SCO offers vast scope for economic cooperation. The

organization is gearing up for regional projects in infrastructure development, energy and communications. In the not-too-distant future, it is set to develop common banking facilities and a common market. An active Indian role at this stage can modulate the processes at work within the SCO in this direction.

Finally, with the right degree of constructive thinking and creativity, Indian diplomacy can aspire to utilise the SCO forum for tempering India's bilateral relations with the organization's member countries and observers. Much more productive diplomacy is possible within the SCO than via any grand Asian conclaves.

An SCO summit meeting in a slightly overgrown town like Bishkek nestled against the foothills of the stunning Pamir Mountains may not be lit up like the Congress of Vienna with 16,000 candles and chandeliers. The SCO transacts its business modestly. It eschews the heady mixture of politics and appetite. But it will be a good forum for India to learn to be an unpretentious team player alongside its own neighbours amongst whom ultimately, after all, it has to live.

CONCLUSION

India's Central Asia policy is at a crossroads. Regrettably, a perceptible "cooling off" is apparent of late in the UPA government's approach towards the SCO. This is also to be seen in the broader context of the increasingly lukewarm attitude that the government has adopted *vis-à-vis* the Russia-China-India trilateral format. Certainly, the fervour with which the UPA government viewed the trilateral dialogue initially already seems a distant memory.

Today, the UPA government hesitates. It shies away from asserting the crucial importance of a democratized and "multipolar" world order. It constantly looks over its shoulder in order to make out how to harmonize its foreign policy orientations with the US global strategy. The American opposition to the SCO and the Russia-China-India format seems to work as a major determinant in the Indian policy. Of course, from the US perspective, SCO and any strategic understanding between the three major Asian power – Russia, China and India – would be an unwelcome development as that would go a long way in strengthening the "multipolarity" of the international system and would pose a hurdle to the US agenda of hegemony, apart from making it all the more difficult for the US to "claw" its way back to the Asia theatre, restoring its Cold War era strategic influence and economic dominance that has suffered significant erosion during the past 15 years due to a variety of factors.

Indian interests in the medium and long term will be served by a constructive approach to the SCO and the Russia-China-India trilateral format. At any rate, Asian unity must remain an axiom of the Indian policies. Certainly, India's interests will not be served in any way whatsoever by partaking of the US stratagem of dividing Asia into rival blocs. India must firmly and categorically reject the American attempt to inject the "cold war mentality" in the Asian region.

The weakening of India's Central Asia policy in the recent years testifies to the grave danger of hitching our wagons to the US regional policies. It remains a matter of utmost concern that once India gets locked into the nuclear deal with the US, New Delhi's capacity to pursue an independent foreign policy will be severely curbed. There is no gainsaying the fact that the so-called Hyde Act legislated by the US Congress is intended to make the Indian foreign policy "congruent" to the US policies. The American side is fairly explicit to the point of being blunt as to what it expects out of India as a "strategic partner."

Without doubt, India's close identification with the US regional policy will work as a negative factor on our Central Asia policy. The heart of the matter is that Central Asia need not be a theatre at all where India must inevitably cross swords with Russian or Chinese interests. The Central Asian steppes are vast enough to allow the legitimate interplay of Russian, Chinese and Indian strategic interests. If only the Indian policy makers would have the sagacity to make use of the SCO forum creatively, enormous scope exists in regional cooperation involving Russia and China. That would be the sure recipe of regional security and stability.

Such a constructive approach on the part of the Indian government, in fact, would even give added impetus to the expansion of our bilateral relations with China in a mutually beneficial and friendly direction. We would do well to remember that the genesis of the SCO lies in the fair, amicable settlement of the longstanding border disputes between China on the one hand and Russia, Kazakhstan, Kyrgyzstan and Tajikistan on the other, which were a bitter legacy of history.

NOTES

COMING OUT OF THE NUCLEAR COLD

[The author would like to acknowledge Dr A. Gopalakrishnan, T. Jayaraman and Sudhanva Deshpande.]

1 International Atomic Energy Agency (IAEA), *Communication of 10 May 2005 received from the Government of Sweden on behalf of the participating Governments of the Nuclear Suppliers Group,* INFCIRC/539/Rev.3 Date: 30 May 2005.

2 http://www.mtcr.info/english/index.html.

3 The Wassenaar arrangement came as a post-Cold War successor to the COCOM export control regime as can be seen from the Genesis of the Wassenaar Arrangement from its official website url: http://www.wassenaar.org/introduction/origins.html.

4 M.R. Srinivasan, R.B. Grover, S.A. Bharadwaj, "Nuclear Power in India: Winds of Change," *Economic and Political Weekly*, December 3, 2005, pp. 5183–88. Though Srinivasan et al. have not talked of the impact of the 1974 sanctions here, they have given an account of the kind of problems faced by DAE in developing technology on the basis of the industrial infrastructure then existing in the country.

5 Non-proliferation Treaty, url: http://www.un.org/events/npt2005/npttreaty.html.

6 "For Tehran, Nuclear Program is a Matter of National Pride," George Perkovich, *Yale Global*, March 21, 2005.

7 As the Prime Minister put it, "our security concerns arising from proliferation activities in our extended neighbourhood have shaped our position." Manmohan Singh, suo moto Statement on India's Iran vote in Parliament, February 17, 2006.

8 Stephen G. Rademaker, former Assistant Secretary, US State Department, stated:

"the best illustration of this is the two votes India cast against Iran at the IAEA," he said, adding: "I am the first person to admit that the votes were coerced." Quoted by Siddharth Varadarajan, "India's anti-Iran votes were coerced," *The Hindu*, February 16, 2007.

9 Joint Statement of George Bush and Manmohan Singh, July 18, 2005, available at http://www.indianembassy.org/press_release/2005/July/21.htm.

10 For details of Left parties' objections, see the documents at http://www.cpim.org/nuclear/09042007-nuclear-deal.htm.

11 For more details on this, see Ninan Koshy's contribution in the present volume.

12 Various writers have commented on the relationship between the Hyde Act and the 123 Agreement. See, among others, articles by Bramha Chellaney and A.Gopalakrishnan in the *Asian Age*.

13 H.R. Conf. Rep. No. 109–721, at 22 (Dec. 7, 2006) Hyde Act Joint Explanatory Statement of the Committee of Conference.

14 "Indeed, by allowing India to be the first and only country in the world to be a *de facto* and *de jure* nuclear power, . . . without having to sign either the NPT or the CTBT, India has been allowed to have its cake and eat it too." Abhishek Manu Singhvi, "N-deal: Need for less fission and more fusion," *Times of India*, September 11, 2007.

15 "An Agreement for Cooperation with India will also be subject to the prospective application of AEA section 129, with July 18, 2005 instead of the NNPA's March 1978 date of enactment as the new 'grandfather' date. . . . The Hyde Act looks beyond India's past nuclear explosives tests and recognises India's nuclear weapons programme as a continuing *fait accompli*. However, in all other respects, it requires India to conform to the conduct required of all other non-nuclear-weapon states with which the US engages in nuclear trade." Jay R. Kraemer and Frank Aum, "The US-India nuclear agreement: progress toward nuclear cooperation with India and a new paradigm in non-proliferation policy," *International Journal of Nuclear Law*, Vol. 1, No. 4, 2007, pp. 418–39.

16 ". . . the 123 Agreement recognises India as a *de facto* nuclear weapons state and for the first time has been granted a *de jure* nuclear weapons state status", Kapil Sibal, "123 Agreement: a response to Brahma Chellaney," *The Hindu*, September 17, 2007. See also Singhvi, note 14 above.

17 H.R. Conf. Rep. No. 109–721, at 22 (Dec. 7, 2006) Hyde Act Joint Explanatory Statement of the Committee of Conference. Emphasis added.

18 Prime Minister Manmohan Singh's Reply to Discussion in Rajya Sabha on Civil Nuclear Energy Cooperation with the United States, New Delhi, August 17, 2006.

19 Clause 103 (b) (4) The Hyde Act

20 PM's Rajya Sabha Statement 17th August, 2006, op cit

21 PM's Statement in Lok Sabha, August 13, 2007, available at http://pib.nic.in/release/release.asp?relid=29793&kwd=.

22 Clause 5.6, 123 Agreement, emphasis added.

23 Clause 6 (iii), 123 Agreement.

24 *Integrated Energy Policy, 2006*, Report of the Expert Committee, Planning Commission of India, New Delhi, available at http://planningcommission.nic.in/reports/genrep/rep_intengy.pdf

25 "Between 1975 and 1989, the average period required to complete a plant soared from 5 years to 12. The bill for a group of 75 first-generation plants totalled $224.1 billion (in current dollars), 219% more than estimated, according to a 1986 Energy Dept. study. In time, many utilities collapsed under these debts even as customers' bills soared." "Nuclear Power's Missing Fuel," *Business Week* magazine, July 10, 2006.

26 Prabir Purkayastha, "Discovering Nuclear Energy for Justifying a Bad Deal," *People's Democracy*, September 2, 2007.

27 "N-deal: Need for less fission and more fusion," Abhishek Manu Singhvi, *Times of India*, September 11, 2007.

28 "US companies clamour to break into India's $100bn nuclear energy sector," Amy Yee, *Financial Times*, November 23, 2006.

29 For a detailed analysis of the Enron fiasco, see Prabir Purkayastha and Vijay Prashad, *Enron Blowout: Corporate Capitalism and the Theft of the Global Commons*, New Delhi: LeftWord, 2002.

30 Some sections of the Indian media have seen a dichotomy between the argument that nuclear power is expensive and Buddhadeb Bhattacharyya's statement that West Bengal is examining a proposal for NPC setting up nuclear power stations in West Bengal. There is, in fact, no dichotomy – the Left has always argued for keeping open the nuclear option and the techno-economics of each proposal will have to be evaluated within the overall context of energy security.

31 Tenth Five Year Plan, Planning Commission.

32 Even Perkovich, no great admirer of the India-US nuclear deal, finds the US attempts to block the Iran-Pakistan pipeline against India's energy interests. "Perversely, the United States is trying to block a highly cost-effective way to get natural gas to India, via an overland pipeline from Iran through Pakistan." George Perkovich, "Faulty Promises: The US-India Nuclear Deal," Policy Outlook No. 21, September 2005, Carnegie Endowment for International Peace.

33 "A World Free of Nuclear Weapons," Prime Minister Rajiv Gandhi at the United Nations General Assembly. New York, June 9, 1988, available at http://www.indianembassy.org/policy/Disarmament/disarm15.htm.

34 J. Thiagarajan, "Completing What NDA Had Begun," *People's Democracy*, October 26, 2007.

35 The *Wall Street Journal* in its issue of January 5, 2007, published a call for nuclear disarmament from four former Cold War veterans of the US, including Henry Kissinger.

INDIA-US NUCLEAR DEAL: THE BROADER PICTURE AND WIDER IMPLICATIONS

1 Veerappa Moily, "The Highest Feat of Diplomacy," *The Hindu,* August 28, 2007.
2 Op-Ed article, *The Times of India*, March 31, 2005.
3 White House, Washington, July 18, 2005. For more details, see Ninan Koshy, *Under the Empire: India's New Foreign Policy*, New Delhi: LeftWord, 2005, chapter 11, "America's Vassal?"
4 Siddharth Varadarajan, "A Farewell to the Gas Pipeline," The Hindu, July 22, 2005.
5 Prime Minister's reply on discussion in Rajya Sabha on Civil Nuclear Cooperation with the USA, *The Hindu,* August 18, 2006.
6 Siddharth Varadarajan, "India Has Little Reason to Cheer," *The Hindu,* December 9, 2006.
7 Prime Minister's reply on discussions in Rajya Sabha.
8 *The Hindustan Times*, 13 December 2006.
9 Rajiv Sikri, "The India-US Nuclear Deal – The Road Ahead," *South Asia Analysis Group,* paper no. 3072, 23.12.2006.
10 White House, Washington, July 18, 2005.
11 Nicholas Burns, "Heady times for India and US," *Washington Post*, April 29, 2007.
12 Ibid.
13 *The Hindu,* May 2, 2007.
14 Statement by Nicholas Burns on July 27, 2007, State Department, Washington.
15 "123 Agreement, an Assault on Nuclear Sovereignty: BJP," *The Hindu*, August 5, 2007.
16 For more details, see Ninan Koshy, *Under the Empire.*
17 Left Parties' Statement on the India-US Bilateral Nuclear Agreement, August 7, 2007.
18 Prime Minister's Statement, "This Agreement does not in any way restrict our strategic autonomy," *The Hindu*, August 14, 2007.
19 Ibid.
20 Siddharth Varadarajan, "A Guide to the Provisions of the 123 Agreement," *The Hindu*, August 4, 2007.
21 Brahma Chellany, "Text and Context," *Asian Age,* August 4, 2007.
22 Statement of the President on HR 5862 the Henry J. Hyde United States-India Peaceful Atomic Energy Cooperation Act of 2006, White House, December 18, 2002.
23 Left Parties' Statement.
24 *The Hindu*, 31 August 2007.
25 Michael Krepon and Alex Stolar, "The 123 Agreement: From Bad to Worse," *The Hindu*, August 25, 2007.
26 Quadrennial Defence Review 2006, *Pentagon Documents*, Washington, February, 2006.

27 Michael Klare, "Containing China: the US's Real Objective," *Asia Times online*, April 20, 2006.
28 Ibid.
29 Condoleeza Rice, "Campaign 2000, Promoting the National Interest," *Foreign Affairs*, January-February 2000.
30 Joint Statement of the US-Japan Security Consultative Committee, Media Note, Department of State, Washington, May 1, 2007.
31 Steven R. Weisman, *New York Times*, March 3, 2006.
32 Paul Richter, *Los Angels Times*, March 4, 2006.
33 *Times of India*, March 3, 2006.
34 Michael Krepon and Alex Stolar, "The 123 Agreement: From Bad to Worse."
35 "Naval Exercises with the US Bad for India: Karat," *Hindustan Times*, September 1, 2007. For the CPI(M)'s view on the emerging India-US strategic alliance and the nuclear deal, see Prakash Karat, *Subordinate Ally: The Nuclear Deal and India-US Strategic Relations*, New Delhi: LeftWord, 2007.

INDIA, CENTRAL ASIA AND THE GREAT GAME

1 Wang Baofu, "Russia no longer shows forbearance," *People's Daily*, 17 July 2007.
2 "Strategic nuclear escalation & the multipolar world," *People's Daily*, 11 July 2007. Emphasis added.
3 "NATO caught in transformation," *People's Daily*, 23 July 2007.
4 "Russia rejects tougher stance on Iran," *The Financial Times*, 13 September 2007.
5 "The US violating rights of Central Asian countries: Broujerdi," *Mehr News Agency*, 15 July 2007.
6 "Editorial: Shanhaeid," *The Financial Times*, 20 August 2007.
7 Kremlin website, 17 August 2007.
8 "Deepening good neighbourliness, spurring common development," *People's Daily*, 20 August 2007.
9 Fu Mengzi, "Signs point to rekindling of Cold War mentality," *China Daily*, 21 August 2007.
10 Fu Mengzi, "Signs point to rekindling of Cold War mentality," *China Daily*, 21 August 2007.
11 "US scheming for 'Great Central Asia' strategy," *People's Daily*, 3 August 2006.
12 Fu Xiaqing, "Taliban phenomenon a grave concern," *People's Daily*, 1 June 2007.
13 "A Survey of Russian Federation Foreign Policy," March 2007, Ministry of Foreign Affairs of the Russian Federation, available at http://www.mid.ru/Brp_4.nsf/arh/89A30B3A6B65B4F2C32572D700292F74?OpenDocument.
14 "Russia to allocate $200 million to Afghan army," *RIA Novosti*, 2 July 2007.
15 Nikolai Khorunzhy, "Afghanistan: staying the course?," *RIA Novosti*, 10 July 2007.
16 "CSTO proposes to SCO joint effort on post-conflict Afghanistan," *RIA Novosti*, 31 July 2007.

17 "Afghans losing hope: former FM and Massoud aide," *AFP*, 9 September 2007.

18 "Taliban ready for talks," *Dawn*, 11 September 2007.

19 Yevgeny Primakov, "Does the US Have its Priorities Right?," *Moscow News*, 12 July, 2007.

20 Alexander Khramchikhin, "The Chinese Detour," *Izvestia*, 20August, 2007.

21 Bates Gill, "Chinese Security Interests and Activities with Central Asian States," paper presented at the US National Defence University Conference, Washington DC, April 2004.

22 Dmitry Kosyrev, "China gives the Korean stalemate a happy ending," *RIA Novosti*, 3 August 2007.